My Lord and My God!

A Scriptural Journey with the Followers of Jesus

W9-ARP-030

My Lord and My God!

A Scriptural Journey with the Followers of Jesus

Jeanne Kun

the WORD®
among us

The Word Among Us
9639 Doctor Perry Road
Ijamsville, Maryland 21754
ISBN:1-59325-051-7
www.wordamongus.org

Copyright © 2004 by The Word Among Us Press
All rights reserved.

Poems *Peter: In Memoriam, Lord, I Am Not Worthy, Faith's Prayer, Zacchaeus' Tall Tale, The Radiance of Faith, Bethany Revisited: My Love's Anointing, The Judas in Me, Laid to Rest, Awakened to Eternity,* and *Graven on the Palms of Your Hands,* copyright © 2004 by Jeanne Kun.
All rights reserved. Used by permission.

Scripture passages are taken from the Revised Standard Version Bible: Catholic Edition, © 1965 and 1966 by the Division of Christian Education of the National Council of the Churches of Christ in the U.S.A.
All rights reserved. Used by permission.

Cover and Book Design: David Crosson
Cover image: *Christ's Charge to Saint Peter* by Raphael (1483-1520)
Location: Victoria and Albert Museum, London, Great Britain
Photo Credit: Victoria and Albert Museum, London/Art Resource, N.Y.

Nihil obstat: The Reverend Michael Morgan, Chancellor
Censor Librorum
December 3, 2004

Imprimatur: +Most Reverend Victor Galeone
Bishop of St. Augustine
December 3, 2004

No part of this publication may be reproduced, stored in a retrieval system, or transmitted in any form or by any means—electronic, mechanical, photocopy, recording, or any other—except brief quotations in printed reviews, without the prior permission of the publisher.

Made and printed in the United States of America.

Library of Congress Cataloging-in-Publication Data

Kun, Jeanne, 1951-
    My Lord and my God! : a scriptural journey with the followers of Jesus / Jeanne Kun.
        p. cm.
    Includes bibliographical references.
    ISBN 1-59325-051-7 (alk. paper)
    1. Bible. N.T.—Biography. 2. Jesus Christ—Friends and associates. 3. Bible. N.T. Gospels—Criticism, interpretation, etc. I. Title.
    BS2430.K86 2005
    226'.0922--dc22   2004023960

Contents

Introduction

May I know you more clearly, love you more dearly, and follow you more nearly, now and forever.

This famous prayer of St. Richard Chicester expresses the ardent desire of every disciple of Christ. Each day, we want to grow in our knowledge and love of the Lord and in our commitment to follow him. *My Lord and My God! A Scriptural Journey with the Followers of Jesus* was written with that goal in mind. We can better follow Jesus when we get to know the men and women who were his first followers. By reflecting on Jesus' encounters with his disciples, we will come to a deeper understanding of our Lord. And, as our knowledge of Jesus increases, so will our love for him and our desire to give our lives each day entirely to him.

My Lord and My God! A Scriptural Journey with the Followers of Jesus is designed to help readers learn to carefully examine the gospels. As we become more attentive and alert to every word and detail written by the evangelists, Jesus and his followers come into sharper focus before our eyes. And as we meditate upon the disciples featured in the ten reflections in this book—among them Simon Peter, Zacchaeus, Bartimaeus, Mary of Bethany, Joseph of Arimathea, Mary Magalene, and Thomas—we'll discover just how diverse the face of discipleship is. In fact, we'll also find our own faces reflected there.

Meeting Jesus and His Followers

Much about Jesus' character is revealed to us in the ways he responded to the people and events in his life. There are so many clues: his words as well as his silences; what he did as well as what he refrained from doing; the actions he praised as well as those he criticized. He taught, healed, affirmed, challenged, and convicted the people he met, calling everyone to a deep transformation of life. These men and women, whether they were rich or poor, learned or simple, esteemed or lowly, Jew or Gentile, related to Jesus in ways that can help us to examine ourselves and our own interactions with our Lord.

As you reflect on each gospel scene, try to get inside the characters yourself. Put yourself in the shoes (or sandals!) of those who encountered Jesus and imagine yourself in the scene. Accompany the woman with the hemorrhage as she pressed through the crowd to reach Jesus and bring him your own needs. Join Mary of Bethany at Jesus' feet and listen to his words to you. Play the role of Judas in your own imagination and realize how close each of us is to succumbing to temptation and betrayal. Go with Mary Magdalene to the garden tomb in her grief and rejoice with her as you, too, encounter the risen Lord there. Like Thomas, stretch out your hand to touch Jesus and, with deepened faith, exclaim, "My Lord and my God!" Or ask yourself where you fit in a particular scene, and which person you identify with right now in your life. As St.

Josemaría Escrivá, the founder of Opus Dei, advised:

> Make it a habit to mingle frequently with the characters who appear in the New Testament. . . . My advice is that, in your prayer, you actually take part in the different scenes of the Gospel, as one more among the people present. . . .
>
> It is not a matter of just thinking about Jesus, of recalling some scenes of his life. We must be completely involved and play a part in his life. We must follow him as closely as Mary his Mother did, as closely as the first twelve, the holy women, the crowds that pressed about him. If we do this without holding back, Christ's words will enter deep into our soul and will really change us.

The men and women who came to Jesus with faith, hope, and love, with needs, weaknesses, and sins, provide a mirror for us. We can see ourselves in their devotion and courage as well as in their anxieties and cares. Look into this mirror and allow God's Spirit to transform you.

How to Use This Book

In *My Lord and My God! A Scriptural Journey with the Followers of Jesus*, we accompany Jesus' followers in the crucial events of their lives. Each chapter focuses on a "scene" as recorded in the New Testament. Carefully read the Scripture narrative—provided in the Catholic edition of the Revised Standard Version—and meditate on it. Also read the accompanying section "Reflecting on the Word" to deepen your understanding of the text.

Two sets of questions are included in each chapter to help you explore the full scope of the passage and consider its relevance to you. Those under the heading "Pondering the Word" require an attentive reading of the Scripture selection and focus on the content and meaning of the text. "Living the Word" questions prompt you to apply the lessons and truths learned through Scripture to your own life.

"Rooted in the Word" offers brief comments on various attributes of the followers of Jesus that are modeled in the corresponding scene. Additional Scripture texts further illustrate the virtue or character trait highlighted in this section. A selection from a Catholic writer—ancient or modern—concludes each chapter. These excerpts, under the heading "Treasuring the Word," are indeed treasures from the Church's rich heritage.

The format of *My Lord and My God! A Scriptural Journey with the Followers of Jesus* is suited to personal reflection and individual study as well as group discussion. In either case, begin each session with prayer, asking God to speak to you through his word.

Although each chapter's Scripture scene is provided in full in this book, you will find it helpful to have a Bible on hand for looking up other passages and cross-references.

Whether you use this book for personal study or as an aid in your prayer time, read at your own pace, taking as much time as you need to meditate on the material and pursue any thoughts it brings to mind. You will gain the most benefit from your study by writing down your answers to the questions in the space provided. End your reading or study with a prayer of thanksgiving to God for what you have learned and ask the Holy Spirit how to apply it to your life.

If you use this book in a Bible study group, it is especially important that each member take the time to prepare well for each session. Read the material decided upon in advance and consider your answers to the questions so the group can have a rewarding discussion in the time allotted. Actively contribute to the discussion, but also listen attentively to the others in the group. Respect each member of the group and their contribution to the discussion. The group might also want to designate a leader or moderator to facilitate the discussion and to include a time of prayer together during the meeting.

"My Lord and my God!" Since Thomas first exclaimed these words twenty centuries ago, millions of men and women have come to meet the risen Lord and repeat this profound profession of faith in him. I pray that *My Lord and My God! A Scriptural Journey with the Followers of Jesus* will help each of us make this proclamation our own.

Jeanne Kun
The Word Among Us

Simon Peter

Put out into the deep and let down your nets for a catch.
Luke 5:4

The spectacular catch of fish was granted by Jesus as a sign of [Simon Peter's] true calling. Just as [he] had caught the miraculous draught of fish through His power, through the same grace [Peter] would draw men into the kingdom of God.
C. Bernard Ruffin, *The Twelve: The Lives of the Apostles After Calvary*

Peter: In Memoriam

Peter,
while through so many cool nights and sunlit days
you cast your nets into Galilee's blue waters
(hauling in the makings of good business),
did you ever imagine
you'd soon be catching men instead of fish?

Follow me, and I will make you fishers of men,
the young rabbi bid you
in words that won your heart.

II
Peter,
when waking on the heights of Tabor,
were you overcome with wonder
at beholding Christ so gloriously transfigured,
his face shining like the blinding sun
and his raiment dazzling white as light?

This is my Son, my chosen; listen to him!
The Father's voice was heard within the cloud
speaking words that thundered in your ears.

III
Peter,
was your pride broken
when the cock crowed at morning's dawn
and, sore with grief and shame,
bitter tears coursed down your cheeks
because you'd denied your Lord not only once but thrice?

Satan demanded to have you, that he might sift you like wheat,
but I have prayed for you that your faith may not fail;
and when you have turned again, strengthen your brethren.
So had your master (his eyes full of understanding) foretold
with words that made you wonder at their meaning.

IV

Peter,
as you traveled through vast lands and across strange seas,
did you marvel at the miracle and mysteries
that led you to proclaim the gospel
so far from familiar shores
and the homey comforts of Capernaum?

Tend my lambs. . . . Feed my sheep.
Thus did the risen Christ commission you
in words that made you shepherd of a worldwide flock.

V

Peter,
surrounded by the seven hills of Rome (and Nero's prison walls),
did you miss the wind blowing on Lake Gennesaret
and the sound of the waves lapping against your fishing boat?
As you awaited a martyr's cross,
did you strain to hear the echo of the Crucified's voice once more?

Truly, truly, I say to you, when you were young,
you girded yourself and walked where you would;
but when you are old, you will stretch out your hands,
and another will gird you and carry you where you do not wish to go.
So had your teacher spoken long ago
these words that told already of your journey's end.

VI

Now, Peter,
having followed in the master's steps so faithfully,
at last you've gained eternity
where there's no longer need
for any prayer or plea but praise
and all God's words are treasured in your heart.

Well done, good and faithful servant.

Luke 5:1-11 The Scene

5:1 While the people pressed upon him to hear the word of God, [Jesus] was standing by the lake of Gennesaret. 2 And he saw two boats by the lake; but the fishermen had gone out of them and were washing their nets. 3 Getting into one of the boats, which was Simon's, he asked him to put out a little from the land. And he sat down and taught the people from the boat. 4 And when he had ceased speaking, he said to Simon, "Put out into the deep and let down your nets for a catch." 5 And Simon answered, "Master, we toiled all night and took nothing! But at your word I will let down the nets." 6 And when they had done this, they enclosed a great shoal of fish; and as their nets were breaking, 7 they beckoned to their partners in the other boat to come and help them. And they came and filled both the boats, so that they began to sink. 8 But when Simon Peter saw it, he fell down at Jesus' knees, saying, "Depart from me, for I am a sinful man, O Lord." 9 For he was astonished, and all that were with him, at the catch of fish which they had taken; 10 and so also were James and John, sons of Zebedee, who were partners with Simon. And Jesus said to Simon, "Do not be afraid; henceforth you will be catching men." 11 And when they had brought their boats to land, they left everything and followed him.

See also Matthew 4:18-22; Mark 1:16-20

Reflecting on the Word

How often God chooses the most improbable people to move forward his purposes! A cowardly Jonah fled from God's commission to preach to the Ninevites (Jonah 1:1-3). Israel's great King David committed adultery (2 Samuel 11:2-5). Again and again God has manifested his power by transforming weakness into strength and sinners into saints. And so God chose a brash fisherman to become his instrument to "catch" men and women for his kingdom (Luke 5:10). For Simon Peter, what began with the invitation to become "fishers of men" (Matthew 4:19) would result in the spreading of Jesus' message far beyond the shores of the Sea of Galilee.

Simon BarJona, that is, son of Jona or John (Matthew 16:17; John 1:42; 21:15), and his brother Andrew were originally from the village of Bethsaida on the northeast side of the Sea of Galilee (John 1:44). At some point they moved to Capernaum on the lake's northwestern shore, where Simon lived with his wife and in-laws (Mark 1:29-30). It's likely that he ran one of the commercial fishing cooperatives that flourished then around the Sea of Galilee (also known as Lake Gennesaret) and sold their catch to local salters and to wholesalers in Jerusalem. Famous throughout the Roman Empire, Galilee's fisheries generated a prosperous export trade.

Now Galilee was astir with the extraordinary deeds of a young rabbi, Jesus of Nazareth, who was going about the region declaring, "The time is fulfilled, and the kingdom of God is at hand; repent, and believe in the gospel" (Mark 1:14-15). One day while Jesus was preaching to the crowd that had gathered near the lake to hear him—so Luke recounted vividly, perhaps drawing on the disciples' own memories—he used Simon's fishing boat as a "floating pulpit." When he ceased teaching, Jesus told Simon, "Put out into the deep and let down your nets for a catch" (Luke 5:1-4).

Simon Peter was an experienced fisherman who knew his business well. He had worked unsuccessfully the whole night—the best time for net fishing—and didn't think that he'd catch anything now. Nonetheless, he did as Jesus directed, saying, "At your word I will let down the nets" (Luke 5:5).

Simon's obedience was remarkably rewarded as he took in a great shoal of fish. So huge was the catch that the nets were breaking, and he beckoned to his partners' boat for help (Luke 5:6-7). Overwhelmed and astonished, Simon "fell down at Jesus' knees, saying, 'Depart from me, for I am a sinful man, O Lord' " (5:8). In his study of the apostles entitled *The Twelve*, C. Bernard Ruffin wrote of the fishermen's reaction: "Peter's awe and that of his companions James and John was so immense that it bordered on fear. They knew the sea well enough to know that there was no natural explanation for their extraordinary catch." A devout Jew, Simon Peter "realized that he was in the presence of a higher being and felt totally inadequate," added Ruffin.

But Jesus calmed Peter's fears—"Do not be afraid" (5:10)—and seemed to simply ignore Peter's declaration that he was a sinful man.

When Jesus called, Simon and his fishing partners left everything—the fresh catch of fish, their boats and nets, even their families. In following Jesus, they entered into a unique personal relationship with him as his disciples and began to participate in his mission.

The miraculous draught of fish was only one of the remarkable experiences that Simon Peter shared with his Lord. Peter, James, and John made up Jesus' intimate circle of followers and were present at the Transfiguration (Matthew 17:1-8), the raising of Jairus' daughter (Luke 8:51-56), and Jesus' prayer at Gethsemane (Mark 14:33-42). Additional events in the gospels show Peter as a man of great love and loyalty, but also one with very human failings. He was the first to acknowledge Jesus as the Messiah and Son of God, and Jesus entrusted to this "rock" the keys of the kingdom (Matthew 16:13-19). But that didn't mean that Peter understood the Lord: Appalled at Jesus' prediction of his passion and death, Peter cried, "God forbid, Lord!" and Jesus sharply corrected him (16:21-23).

By nature Peter was bold and confident, proud and outspoken. He frequently acted impetuously, as when he exclaimed, "Lord, if it is you, bid me come to you on the water" (Matthew 14:28). "Lord, I am ready to go with you to prison and to death," he rashly boasted (Luke 22:33). Then he was quick to reverse his brash assertion under pressure, claiming, "I do not know the man" (Matthew 26:72). Indeed, a fearful Peter denied knowing Jesus not only once but three times. Art historian Sr. Wendy Beckett wrote of Peter's fall:

> Will he lose all heart, perhaps even kill himself, as Judas did (another man wracked by grief)? But while Judas felt only remorse, which consumed itself in pointless repining, Peter feels contrition, a healing sorrow that will lead to repentance and a change of heart. (*Sister Wendy's Nativity*)

When the cock crowed and Jesus looked at him (Luke 22:60-61), Peter realized again—as he had earlier in Galilee—that he was a sinful man. But he also knew that Jesus loved him unconditionally, and his humility saved him from despairing of forgiveness. We can learn from Peter to face our sins and failings humbly and cling to the Lord: "Peter shows us how to respond to our inevitable stumbles and falls along the way: by accepting the grace to pick ourselves up, stick close to Jesus, and exchange self-reliance for trust in God" (Louise Perrotta, "From Fisherman to Friend of God").

After the resurrection, Jesus encountered Peter again at the Sea of Galilee. There the risen Lord provided his fishermen-disciples with another wondrous haul of fish (John 21:1-14). There too he gently probed the heart of the man who had denied him, three times asking "Do you love me?" and calling from his humbled friend a new declaration of love. Accepting Peter's affirmations—"Lord, you know everything; you know that I love you"—Jesus entrusted to him the work of shepherding his flock: "Feed my lambs. . . . Tend my sheep" (21:15-17).

Filled with the Spirit at Pentecost, Peter proclaimed the gospel far and wide and cared for the fledging church. During the final years of his life, the chief apostle—"the rock"— headed the Christian community in Rome and, true to his master's call to the end, was martyred there during the reign of the emperor Nero. Even with his imperfections, Peter faithfully fulfilled the commission Jesus had given him.

Becoming a follower of Jesus led Simon Peter on many journeys, but the most significant one was, as author Louise Perrotta noted, "his inner journey of transformation from . . . one who was convinced of his own strength to one who learned that he could only please the Lord as he learned to draw strength from Jesus, his beloved Master." We are called to be disciples of the same master as Peter was—and we can do much for the Lord if we, like the fisherman-apostle, acknowledge that we are not perfect and rely on the Holy Spirit at work in us.

Pondering the Word

1. What does it mean to follow Jesus and become his disciple, according to Luke 5:1-11? What does this passage tell you about Jesus' mission and ministry?

_____

_____

_____

_____

_____

_____

_____

_____

_____

2. What insights do Peter's actions and statements as described in this scene give you into his character and personality? What adjectives would you use to describe Peter?

_____

_____

_____

_____

_____

_____

_____

_____

_____

3. The miraculous catch was a theophany—a manifestation of God's glory and power. Why do you think Jesus used this particular miracle to issue his call to Peter, Andrew, James, and John?

_____

_____

_____

_____

_____

_____

_____

_____

4. Jesus gave Simon the name Peter, which means "rock" (Matthew 16:18). In the Old Testament, God gave Abram the new name Abraham (Genesis 17:1-8) and Jacob the new name Israel (35:9-12). What is the significance of a new name? Why do you think Jesus gave Simon his new name?

_____

_____

_____

_____

_____

_____

_____

_____

_____

5. Based on Matthew 16:13-19 and John 21:15-17, summarize in your own words the role and responsibility Jesus entrusted to Peter in the Church. How did Peter carry out Jesus' commission to him?

_____

_____

_____

_____

_____

_____

_____

_____

6. John the Evangelist also recorded a scene in his Gospel that included a miraculous catch of fish (John 21:1-14). What similarities and differences do you see between Luke's account and John's? Why do you think John closed his Gospel with this event?

_____

_____

_____

_____

_____

_____

_____

_____

_____

_____

_____

Living the Word

1. After Peter witnessed the miracle of the great catch of fish, he said to Jesus, "Depart from me, for I am a sinful man, O Lord" (Luke 5:8). Can you think of a time when you encountered the Lord and felt as Peter did? What did you do about it?

_____

_____

_____

_____

_____

_____

_____

_____

2. Is there anything you have "left behind" in your life in order to follow Jesus more closely? Is there anything the Lord is currently asking you to change or give up to be his disciple?

_____

_____

_____

_____

_____

_____

_____

_____

_____

_____

_____

_____

3. With which of Simon Peter's character traits would you most closely identify yourself? Why?

_____

_____

_____

_____

_____

_____

_____

_____

4. Is there a particular ministry you feel that the Lord has called you to carry out as his disciple? If so, how successful do you think you have been in carrying out this ministry? What has helped or hindered you?

_____

_____

_____

_____

_____

_____

_____

_____

_____

_____

_____

_____

5. How is your relationship with Jesus connected to your participation in his mission?

_____

_____

_____

_____

_____

_____

_____

6. What have you learned from Peter's responses to Jesus that will help you in your own personal and spiritual growth?

_____

_____

_____

_____

_____

_____

_____

_____

_____

Peter: A Portrait of Discipleship

When Jesus called, Simon Peter immediately left everything to follow him. Yet it was only slowly, step by step, that Peter came to understand the full meaning of being a disciple of Jesus and the full cost of following him unreservedly.

As Father George Montague, S.M., noted in his commentary, *Mark: Good News for Hard Times*:

> The disciples learn the lessons of Jesus by living with him. . . . Christian education, as done by Jesus, is no mere head-trip! It is a lived experience. Secondly, there is no address for Jesus' school, no fixed place where the disciples gather daily to be taught. Jesus is constantly on the move. Discipleship is a journey. Thirdly, Jesus provides no map to tell his disciples where they will be tomorrow. Discipleship is following Jesus wherever he decides to go now. It is to give Jesus control of the journey.

After Pentecost, Peter spent the rest of his life faithfully fulfilling his master's call. Empowered by the Holy Spirit, he boldly proclaimed the good news, worked miracles and healings in the name of Jesus, endured imprisonment and persecution for the sake of the gospel, and guided the church through its early formative years. The fisherman-apostle from Galilee was martyred in Rome around A.D. 64. An ancient tradition holds that because he felt unworthy of imitating Jesus in his death, Simon Peter was, at his own request, crucified upside down.

No less than Peter are we, too, called to follow Jesus unconditionally. Nor do we walk this path alone, for Jesus himself accompanies us each step of the way, just as he accompanied his first disciples.

Read and prayerfully reflect on these additional Scripture passages that portray examples of discipleship and its cost:

> Jesus told his disciples, "If any man would come after me, let him deny himself and take up his cross and follow me. For whoever would save his life will lose it, and whoever loses his life for my sake will find it. For what will it profit a man, if he gains the whole world and forfeits his life? Or what shall a man give in return for his life? For the Son of man is to come with his angels in the glory of his Father, and then he will repay every man for what he has done." (Matthew 16:24-27)

> As they were going along the road, a

man said to him, "I will follow you wherever you go." And Jesus said to him, "Foxes have holes, and birds of the air have nests; but the Son of man has nowhere to lay his head." To another he said, "Follow me." But he said, "Lord, let me first go and bury my father." But he said to him, "Leave the dead to bury their own dead; but as for you, go and proclaim the kingdom of God." Another said, "I will follow you, Lord; but let me first say farewell to those at my home." Jesus said to him, "No one who puts his hand to the plow and looks back is fit for the kingdom of God." (Luke 9:57-62)

Now great multitudes accompanied [Jesus]; and he turned and said to them, "If any one comes to me and does not hate his own father and mother and wife and children and brothers and sisters, yes, and even his own life, he cannot be my disciple. Whoever does not bear his own cross and come after me, cannot be my disciple. For which of you, desiring to build a tower, does not first sit down and count the cost, whether he has enough to complete it? Otherwise, when he has laid a foundation, and is not able to finish, all who see it begin to mock him, saying, 'This man began to build, and was not able to finish.' Or what king, going to encounter another king in war, will not sit down first and take counsel whether he is able with ten thousand to meet him who comes against him with twenty thousand? And if not, while the other is yet a great way off, he sends an embassy and asks terms of peace. So therefore, whoever of you does not renounce all that he has cannot be my disciple." (Luke 14:25-33)

A ruler asked [Jesus], "Good Teacher, what shall I do to inherit eternal life?" And Jesus said to him, "Why do you call me good? No one is good but God alone. You know the commandments: 'Do not commit adultery, Do not kill, Do not steal, Do not bear false witness, Honor your father and mother.'" And he said, "All these I have observed from my youth." And when Jesus heard it, he said to him, "One thing you still lack. Sell all that you have and distribute to the poor, and you will have treasure in heaven; and come, follow me." (Luke 18:18-22)

Christ also suffered for you, leaving you an example, that you should follow in his steps. (1 Peter 2:21)

Treasuring the Word

A Reading from *Woman Un-Bent* by Irene Zimmerman, O.S.F.

Peter's Call to Discipleship
[Peter is narrating the story.]

We docked our boats close to where the Master was talking and started to clean our nets. I guess Andrew felt as tired as I did, after spending the whole night out there without catching a thing. We didn't pay much attention to him at first. But he had a kind voice, and what he was saying helped me get my thoughts off the awful night we'd had, even though he sounded pretty idealistic.

The usual crowd of cripples, beggars, women, kids, and old folks were around him. He must have just finished a story. If there was anything people liked about him, it was his storytelling. You know you've got a good storyteller when the kids keep still. I never in my life saw so many kids keep still together.

I was untangling the last of the seaweed from our net when I heard him say, "Therefore I tell you, do not worry about your life, what you will eat, or about your body, what you will wear. For life is more than food, and the body more than clothing." I got rid of the seaweed, but it was harder to shake his words loose. "That's easy enough to say," I thought, "but he should try telling my wife that."

Just about then he stopped talking and looked toward us. When I saw how tired he was and how the crowd was pushing and shoving, I motioned to our boat. He nodded and came over.

Andrew and I towed him away from the shore a bit and jumped aboard. I was planning to take him out into the lake so he could rest—maybe get a little sleep. But the Master looked at the birds flying around our boat and started talking to the crowd again.

"Consider the ravens: they neither sow nor reap, they have neither storehouse nor barn, and yet God feeds them," he said. "Of how much more value are you than the birds!"

Some of that made sense, I thought. Even with her worst headache, my mother-in-law would probably agree I was worth more than her pigeons. But it had been a while since the skies rained down manna. I wasn't exactly ready to believe that the Lord was about to put fish on my table without a lot of help from me.

Jesus was still talking. "Do not keep striving for what you are to eat and what you are to drink, and do not keep worrying. . . . Instead, strive for your Father's kingdom, and these things will be given to you as well."

He looked straight at me then. I thought he'd wound up his talk and wanted us to take him farther out. But he added, looking toward the shore again, "Do not be afraid, little flock, for it is your Father's good pleasure to give you the kingdom."

Everybody stood there, perfectly still. I tell you, he had a power about him. The way he talked about God as his Father made you think God really cared if you lived or died—maybe even cared if you didn't catch any fish. So when the Master turned back to me and said, "Put out into the deep water, and let down your nets for a catch," I told him, "Master, we have worked all night long but have caught nothing. Yet if you say so, I will let down the nets."

Well, as soon as our nets hit the water, there was a ruckus you wouldn't believe. I never saw so many fish! They were actually jumping out of the water, trying to get to the nets. Luckily for us, John and James were coming in just then. We called them over to help us before our nets broke.

Even after we'd thrown the smaller fish back, both our boats were full. I looked at all those fish and thought about what the Master had told us—that God really cares if people go hungry or have nothing to put on. All at once I got scared. Who was this man, calling God "Father" and pulling off a miracle like that? I got down on my knees right there in the middle of all those fish—I didn't care what Andrew or James or John thought—and begged him, "Go away from me, Lord, for I am a sinful man!"

And then something happened that for me was an even bigger miracle. Jesus took my hand and looked at me without saying a word. He didn't have to—I knew exactly what he was thinking. "You're a sinful man, all right, Simon," he was telling me. "You talk too much, too quick, and too loud. But when you talk, people pay attention. If you tell them to listen to me, they'll say, 'Simon wouldn't lose his head over some wild-eyed preacher who's really a tax collector in disguise.' You aren't perfect, but I can use you. Will you follow me?"

When Jesus finally dropped my hand, I felt changed. Oh, I knew I could still clean nets and handle a boat. But he was offering me his own power and goodness. And I could either use them to touch other people, even to make those cripples on shore able to walk home on their own two feet if he wanted me to, or I could refuse him. But if I said no to him, I'd be my same old self for the rest of my life.

He said aloud then, talking to the four of us, "Do not be afraid; from now on you will be catching people."

We took the boats in and left them there, with all those fish still wiggling in them. We could do nothing else. He had asked us to follow him.

The Centurion of Capernaum

I tell you, not even in Israel have I found such faith.
Luke 7:9

I am not worthy that Thou should come under my roof; but speak the word only, and [my servant] shall be healed. By calling himself unworthy, [the centurion] showed himself worthy for Christ to come not into his house, but into his heart. Nor would he have said this with so great faith and humility, had he not borne Him in his heart, of whose coming into his house he was afraid. For it were no great happiness for the Lord Jesus to enter into his house, and yet not to be in his heart.
St. Augustine, *Sermons on Selected Lessons of the New Testament*, XII

Lord, I Am Not Worthy

Lord, I am not worthy.

With the startling humility
of one who knows himself in truth
and with faith so bold and sure that you marveled,
the centurion won your favor, Lord,
(and your praise as well).

I too have found grace
(and the largesse of your favor)
as often as I've followed suit
and made his plea my own:

Lord, I am not worthy.

Now I am wholly in debt to you,
for there is no just nor fair return
that I can make, O Lord,
for all your kindnesses to me:
not for the abundant mercies tender and severe
you've shown to me,
nor for pardon granted me
(that plenteous redemption releasing me from all my sin),
nor for provision
you so wisely weigh and measure to my need.

Lord, I am not worthy.

Unequal is the gift I bring to you
for all these gifts you've given me,
and yet I offer all I have:
my gratitude and gladness,
the tribute of a humbled heart.

Lord, I am not worthy.

7:1 After [Jesus] had ended all his sayings in the hearing of the people he entered Capernaum. 2 Now a centurion had a slave who was dear to him, who was sick and at the point of death. 3 When he heard of Jesus, he sent to him elders of the Jews, asking him to come and heal his slave. 4 And when they came to Jesus, they besought him earnestly, saying, "He is worthy to have you do this for him, 5 for he loves our nation, and he built us our synagogue." 6 And Jesus went with them. When he was not far from the house, the centurion sent friends to him, saying to him, "Lord, do not trouble yourself, for I am not worthy to have you come under my roof; 7 therefore I did not presume to come to you. But say the word, and let my servant be healed. 8 For I am a man set under authority, with soldiers under me: and I say to one, 'Go,' and he goes; and to another, 'Come,' and he comes; and to my slave, 'Do this,' and he does it." 9 When Jesus heard this he marveled at him, and turned and said to the multitude that followed him, "I tell you, not even in Israel have I found such faith." 10 And when those who had been sent returned to the house, they found the slave well.

See also Matthew 8:5-13

Reflecting on the Word

Jesus worked an amazing miracle that day in Capernaum when he healed a man who was close to death. But what is most remarkable and unprecedented in this scene is the trusting faith of the man's master, a foreign officer highly esteemed by the town's Jewish leaders.

When Jesus began his ministry in Galilee, he made Capernaum his adopted home and "base of operations" (Matthew 4:13; Mark 2:1). Capernaum was also home to many fishermen, among them Peter and his family (Mark 1:21, 29), since it lay on the northwest shore of the Sea of Galilee. Most likely, Jesus stayed in Peter's house when he was not on the road preaching and teaching throughout the region. Capernaum was situated on the border of Galilee and an international highway, the Via Maris, passed close by, so there was a customs house or tax office (Matthew 9:1, 9; Mark 2:1, 13-14) and military garrison on the outskirts of town.

Herod Antipas governed Galilee as Rome's representative and was responsible for maintaining peace in the province. The imperial Roman army did not keep a legion stationed in Palestine at the time, so order was enforced with an auxiliary peacekeeping contingent, comprised of several cohorts of infantry and a wing of cavalry. The garrison near Capernaum was probably manned by mercenary soldiers recruited from as near as Syria and Phrygia and as far away as Gaul; Jews were exempted from local recruitment under a treaty between Herod and Rome. Auxiliary centurions were either Roman citizens transferred from the legions or noncitizens promoted from the ranks. No matter what their nationality, these officers were to exercise the empire's "Romanizing" influence wherever they were posted and maintain good relations with the locals.

Polybius, a Greek historian of Rome, wrote that centurions "are required not to be bold and adventurous so much as good leaders, of steady and prudent mind, not prone to take the offensive or start fighting wantonly, but able when overwhelmed and hard-pressed to stand fast and die at their post" (*History*, Book VI, 24). From this description, we can form a vivid picture of a centurion. Luke's account of the behavior of the officer in Capernaum personalizes this picture and adds depth to it. In all his actions, this centurion showed himself to be a man of character.

In a time when it was normal for Israelites to despise their foreign occupiers, this man was well thought of by the Jewish elders and had won their high regard. He was also generous, for he had supported the building of the synagogue in Capernaum (Luke 7:3-5). Though a Gentile, perhaps he was a "God-fearer," one who respected or even worshiped the God of Israel. Moreover, the centurion was kind and humane. He was genuinely concerned for his slave's welfare when it was typical for many masters to treat slaves as disposable goods. Most probably, the sick man was the centurion's personal attendant, similar to a British officer's batman. Luke used the Greek word *entimos*—"very dear" or "highly valued"—to describe the slave. It connotes something that is precious, suggesting that the centurion not only valued his servant for his usefulness but thought of him with esteem and respect.

Self-effacing and aware that he was a foreigner, the centurion sent Capernaum's Jewish elders to ask the extraordinary rabbi he had heard so much about to heal his servant (Luke 7:3). In his humility, he didn't address Jesus in person, but relied on others to intercede on his behalf. The elders presented his request, reinforcing it with their own testimony to the centurion's merit: "He is worthy to have you do this for him, for he loves our nation, and he built us our synagogue" (7:4-5). Jesus then set out with them for the centurion's house (7:6).

The centurion must have realized that Jesus couldn't enter a Gentile's home without becoming ritually unclean (see John 19:28; Acts 11:2-3). Thus, in deference to the Mosaic law and Jewish sensibilities, he refrained from placing Jesus in an awkward or embarrassing situation. Moreover, he was considerate and unassuming, and didn't want to impose on Jesus. So he sent a second delegation—this time of friends—to intercept Jesus outside the house with this message: "Lord, do not trouble yourself, for I am not worthy to have you come under my roof; therefore I did not presume to come to you" (Luke 7:6-7).

But it's in the rest of the centurion's message that we see the most noteworthy of all his virtues, his faith: "But say the word, and let my servant be healed. For I am a man set under authority, with soldiers under me: and I say to one, 'Go,' and he goes; and to another, 'Come,' and he comes; and to my slave, 'Do this,' and he does it" (Luke 7:7-9).

The centurion didn't present his merits or assert how deserving he might be of Jesus' help as the elders had. Rather, wrote St. Ambrose, a Father of the Church, "laying aside his military pride [he] puts on humility, being both willing to believe and eager to honor. . . . For by the power not of man, but of God, he supposed that health was given to man." Being a subordinate under a commander as well as an officer with men under his own command, the centurion reasoned and acted on the basis of his professional experience. Accustomed to the dictates of authority and obedience, he firmly believed in the effective power of the spoken word of command. Convinced of what he had heard about Jesus' power over disease and illness, the centurion related to him with faith and confidence. He knew that Jesus had only to say the word—even from a distance, outside the house—and his servant would be healed.

The centurion's logic and the maturity of his faith were remarkable. He recognized that Jesus had authority over sickness and consequently concluded that Jesus was one sent by God and empowered by him. He further reasoned that, since Jesus exercised

God's power, he was acting under and with the authority of God. This Gentile realized what the Jewish scribes and Pharisees had questioned (Luke 5:21-24) and what even the chief priests later failed to perceive when they asked "By what authority are you doing these things, and who gave you this authority?" (Matthew 21:23).

Jesus marveled at the centurion's faith, noting how it surpassed that of the Jews, many of whom vehemently rejected Jesus: "I tell you, not even in Israel have I found such faith" (Luke 7:9). Matthew's account offers this addition to Jesus' commendation of the centurion: "Many will come from east and west and sit at table with Abraham, Isaac, and Jacob in the kingdom of heaven, while the sons of the kingdom will be thrown into the outer darkness" (Matthew 8:11-12). This is an allusion to the feast promised in the messianic age (Isaiah 25:6-9) and to the covenant promise to Abraham and the patriarchs that all nations would share in his blessings (Genesis 12:2-3; 17:1-8). As Archbishop Fulton Sheen noted, "This first pagan who received praise from Our Divine Lord for his faith was one of 'those children of God' scattered abroad in the world who were eventually to be brought into unity through the Redemption" (*Life of Christ*). Thus, in this scene we see a foreshadowing of the universality of the gospel: All people, from every nation and race, of every age and condition, are offered salvation through Christ and are called to follow him.

Jesus honored the centurion's faith and fulfilled his request: "When those who had been sent returned to the house, they found the slave well" (Luke 7:10). *Hygiainon*— "well"—is a strong expression in Greek and describes a vigorous and robust physical condition. According to Luke, the slave had been at the point of death (7:2), and Matthew described him as "lying paralyzed . . . , in terrible distress" (Matthew 8:6). Jesus simply spoke a word, and the man was healed "at that very moment" (8:13). Such marvelous healings were evidence that God was visiting his people (Luke 7:16)!

Neither Luke nor Matthew gave us a name by which we can remember the centurion. But so profound was this man's humility and faith that we remember and repeat his words each time we prepare our hearts to receive Communion: "Lord, I am not worthy to receive you, but only say the word and I shall be healed." And, since the centurion remained unnamed, each of us can more easily put ourselves in his place—and follow his example as we cry out to Jesus.

Pondering the Word

1. How do you think being a professional soldier shaped the centurion's character? His general outlook on life? His behavior toward the Jews in whose town he was stationed?

_____

_____

_____

_____

_____

_____

_____

_____

2. Does the description of the centurion that the Jewish elders gave to Jesus surprise you? Why or why not?

_____

_____

_____

_____

_____

_____

_____

_____

_____

3. This is the only scene in the New Testament in which we read that Jesus "marveled" at a person's faith (Luke 7:9; Matthew 8:10). What do you think it was that most impressed Jesus about the centurion? What additional light does Mark 6:6 cast on Jesus' attitude toward faith and unbelief?

_____

_____

_____

_____

_____

_____

_____

_____

4. What is the connection between faith and humility? How does an attitude of humility foster the growth of faith?

_____

_____

_____

_____

_____

_____

_____

5. What does this story suggest to you about the value of intercessory prayer?

_____

_____

_____

_____

_____

_____

_____

_____

6. Cornelius was a Gentile centurion who also exhibited faith in God's word (Acts 10:1-48). What qualities can you detect in both Cornelius and the centurion of Capernaum that made them so open to God's power and action in their lives?

_____

_____

_____

_____

_____

_____

_____

_____

_____

Living the Word

1. How have you experienced the power of Jesus' word in your life? Think of a time when you were content to take Jesus at his word like the centurion. What happened? What happened when you became anxious for proof that he would act?

_____

_____

_____

_____

_____

_____

_____

_____

2. Which of the centurion's qualities would you most like to imitate? What might help you to do this?

_____

_____

_____

_____

_____

_____

_____

3. What is your attitude toward authority in general? How does this affect your attitude toward God's authority in your life?

_____

_____

_____

_____

_____

_____

_____

_____

_____

4. The Lord wants us to approach him with both humility and confidence. Do you find this difficult? Why or why not?

_____

_____

_____

_____

_____

_____

_____

_____

_____

5. Can you think of an instance when you interceded for someone and saw God's answer to your prayers? How did this affect you?

_____

_____

_____

_____

_____

_____

_____

_____

_____

6. Matthew adds the detail that the centurion's servant was paralyzed (Matthew 8:6). Is there any area of your life in which you feel "paralyzed" spiritually—perhaps by fear or discouragement—and unable to respond to what God is offering to you or asking of you? How can the centurion's example help you?

_____

_____

_____

_____

_____

_____

_____

_____

_____

Rooted in the Word

The Centurion: A Portrait of Humility

The centurion didn't presume that he deserved Jesus' attention or that it was due him. Instead, he approached Jesus with genuine humility.

True humility does not mean having low self-esteem or a poor self-image. It is, rather, a realization of who we are in relation to God. When Isaiah had a vision of the all-holy Lord in the Temple, he cried, "Woe is me! . . . For I am a man of unclean lips, and I dwell in the midst of a people of unclean lips; for my eyes have seen the King, the LORD of hosts!" (Isaiah 6:5). John the Baptist declared that he was not worthy to untie the thong of Jesus' sandals (Mark 1:7). When Peter recognized God's power manifested at the miraculous catch of fish, he implored Jesus, "Depart from me, for I am a sinful man, O Lord" (Luke 5:8).

When we experience the presence and the power of the living God, we realize that nothing about us makes us deserving of his grace—not our accomplishments, wealth, social status, intellect, beauty, or even good deeds. God knows of our unworthiness, and yet he loves us and shows us mercy, which is "undeserved favor": "By grace you have been saved through faith; and this is not your own doing, it is the gift of God—not because of works, lest any man should boast" (Ephesians 2:8-9).

It is with humility that we recognize our dependency on God and his mercy. Yet our humility should go beyond this recognition: We are to imitate the example of Christ himself, "who, though he was in the form of God, did not count equality with God a thing to be grasped, but emptied himself, taking the form of a servant, being born in the likeness of men. And being found in human form he humbled himself and became obedient unto death, even death on a cross" (Philippians 2:6-8).

Read and prayerfully reflect on these additional Scripture passages that describe true humility and its fruits:

Thus says the LORD: "This is the man to whom I will look, he that is humble and contrite in spirit, and trembles at my word." (Isaiah 66:2)

[Jesus said:] "Whoever humbles himself like this child, he is the greatest in the kingdom of heaven." (Matthew 18:4)

[Jesus said:] "He who is greatest among you shall be your servant; whoever exalts himself will be humbled, and whoever humbles himself will be exalted." (Matthew 23:11-12)

[Jesus] also told this parable to some who trusted in themselves that they were righteous and despised others: "Two men went up into the temple to pray, one a Pharisee and the other a tax collector. The Pharisee stood and prayed thus with himself, 'God, I thank thee that I am not like other men, extortioners, unjust, adulterers, or even like this tax collector. I fast twice a week, I give tithes of all that I get.' But the tax collector, standing far off, would not even lift up his eyes to heaven, but beat his breast, saying, 'God, be merciful to me a sinner!' I tell you, this man went down to his house justified rather than the other; for every one who exalts himself will be humbled, but he who humbles himself will be exalted." (Luke 18:9-14)

Do nothing from selfishness or conceit, but in humility count others better than yourselves. Let each of you look not only to his own interests, but also to the interests of others. (Philippians 2:3-4)

Clothe yourselves, all of you, with humility toward one another, for "God opposes the proud, but gives grace to the humble." Humble yourselves therefore under the mighty hand of God, that in due time he may exalt you. (1 Peter 5:5-6)

Without having seen him you love him; though you do not now see him you believe in him and rejoice with unutterable and exalted joy. As the outcome of your faith you obtain the salvation of your souls. (1 Peter 1:8-9)

Treasuring the Word

A Reading from a Homily by Abbot John Eudes Bamberger, O.C.S.O.
Given on the Feast of St. John Chrysostom, September 13, 1999, at the Abbey of the Genesee

"Lord, I Am Not Worthy"

Lord, I am not worthy that you should enter under my roof; say but the word and my soul shall be healed. This text, slightly modified from today's Gospel, is very familiar to all of us since we repeat it daily just before receiving Communion. Whereas in the Gospel it is the centurion's servant whose healing is sought, at Communion we ask that our soul be cured. We intend it chiefly as an expression of humility, aware as we are that the Lord who comes to us in the Eucharist is the all-holy, sinless Son of God. Jesus described these words, however, as an expression of remarkable faith in his person. He found in them, accordingly, an irresistible appeal to his compassion. Certainly both attitudes, humility and faith, are manifested when anyone makes this prayer from the heart and with attention to their meaning. It is awareness of the holiness of our Lord that causes us to be more conscious of our own sinfulness. It is in light of his surpassing purity that our dullness of heart and spiritual insensitivity reveal themselves to us and render us more keenly aware of his condescension in coming to us in Communion. . . .

Since we are created for union with this transcendent holy God, we need greater purity than we can attain to without special graces from the Lord. It is not enough, however, to be aware of our need for grace and healing. We must also have faith and trust that the Lord is well-disposed toward us. The centurion in his request to Jesus expresses a firm faith and confidence in him: "Say but the word and my servant shall be healed." St. John Chrysostom carried this confidence and faith even further. He believed that Jesus surely has the spiritual power to heal us from our moral and spiritual miseries as well as our physical sicknesses, for he is the one to whom all power in heaven and earth was given by the Father. He has merited the grace of reconciliation with the Father whose honor was so offended by our sin. He is our mediator and intercessor with the Father. . . .

Let us too be confident that the Lord loves us and so is ready to heal us so long as we draw near to him with faith and desire to be made pleasing to him. The Eucharist is surely one of the most convincing proofs of his personal love for each of his faithful. As we offer [the Eucharist], may we stir up our faith in his healing power and surrender our hearts to him with confidence that he who so loved us as to die on our behalf will not refuse his mercy to us when we ask that we might be made worthy of his loving presence both now and for all ages to come.

The Woman with the Hemorrhage

If I touch even his garments, I shall be made well.
Mark 5:28

She touched the hem of his garment, she approached him in a spirit of faith, she believed, and she realized that she was cured. . . . So we too, if we wish to be saved, should reach out in faith to touch the garment of Christ.
St. Ambrose, *Exposition Evangelii sec. Lucam,* VI, 56, 58

Faith's Prayer

At times
I have no words
to pray to you.

And then,
simply being in your company,
breathing in the fragrance of your presence
or stretching out my hand to touch your garment's hem,
is prayer enough.

5:24 A great crowd followed [Jesus] and thronged about him. 25 And there was a woman who had had a flow of blood for twelve years, 26 and who had suffered much under many physicians, and had spent all that she had, and was no better but rather grew worse. 27 She had heard the reports about Jesus, and came up behind him in the crowd and touched his garment. 28 For she said, "If I touch even his garments, I shall be made well." 29 And immediately the hemorrhage ceased; and she felt in her body that she was healed of her disease. 30 And Jesus, perceiving in himself that power had gone forth from him, immediately turned about in the crowd, and said, "Who touched my garments?" 31 And his disciples said to him, "You see the crowd pressing around you, and yet you say, 'Who touched me?'" 32 And he looked around to see who had done it. 33 But the woman, knowing what had been done to her, came in fear and trembling and fell down before him, and told him the whole truth. 34 And he said to her, "Daughter, your faith has made you well; go in peace, and be healed of your disease."

See also Matthew 9:20-22; Luke 8:43-48

Reflecting on the Word

Imagine how discouraged this woman must have felt! For twelve years she had futilely sought a cure for her bleeding disorder, only to be disappointed time and time again (Mark 5:25). She had spent all her money on doctor after doctor, but had only gotten worse (5:26). Yet what tremendous faith she exhibited when she reached out to Jesus in her distress!

Jesus' healing of the woman with the hemorrhage is one of many instances in which he showed concern for women. In fact, Matthew, Mark, and Luke all relate that this encounter occurred while Jesus was on his way to help Jairus' daughter, whom he raised from the dead (Matthew 9:18-25; Mark 5:21-43; Luke 8:40-56). He also healed Peter's mother-in-law of a fever (Mark 1:29-31), showed his compassion for the widow of Nain by restoring her only son to life (Luke 7:11-18), and straightened the bent back of a woman who had suffered from her deformity for eighteen years (13:10-17). He treated the woman caught in adultery with mercy and kindness as he encouraged her to sin no more (John 8:2-11), freed Mary Magdalene from the demonic influences that plagued her (Luke 8:2), and enjoyed deep friendship with Martha and her sister Mary (10:38-42; John 11:1-3; 12:1-3). Women were among Jesus' most dedicated followers (Luke 8:2-3; Matthew 27:55-56), and it was to them that he first showed himself after the resurrection (Matthew 28:1-10; Mark 16:1-10; Luke 24:1-11; John 20:11-18).

Scripture commentators describe this woman's physical ailment in various ways. Whatever its cause, the disorder was chronic—and surely quite unpleasant. Besides the pain and inconvenience the woman suffered from such steady bleeding, she probably experienced weakness, weight loss, and anemia. No medical treatment relieved her symptoms or cured her.

Much more than this woman's physical well-being was affected by her condition. According to Mosaic law, a woman was considered "unclean" each month for seven days during the "regular discharge from her body" (Leviticus 15:19). The purpose of this law was not to demean or disparage women; rather, it reflected the high regard the Israelites had for the sacredness of life, and for a woman's contact with that sacredness in reproduction. But the nature of the ailment of the woman in this gospel scene—a continuous flow of blood—would have rendered her constantly unclean nonetheless:

If a woman has a discharge of blood for many days, not at the time of her impurity, or if she has a discharge beyond the time of her impurity, all the days of the discharge she shall continue in uncleanness; as in the days of her impurity, she shall be unclean. Every bed on which she lies, all the days of her discharge, shall be to her as the bed of her impurity; and everything on which she sits shall be unclean, as in the uncleanness of her impurity. And whoever touches these things shall be unclean, and shall wash his clothes, and bathe himself in water, and be unclean until the evening. (Leviticus 15:25-27)

If this woman was relatively young, it's quite likely that her condition would have made marriage and childbearing impossible. If she was already married and had borne children before the onset of her disorder, its chronic nature would have severely restricted her contact with her husband and family and curtailed her activities. Regardless of her age or marital status, her continual "uncleanness" would have cut her off from her friends, since any contact with her would have made them ritually unclean, too. Moreover, she was isolated from participation in the public worship of God.

This woman "had heard the reports about Jesus" (Mark 5:27). Encouraged by stories of how he had healed so many people of diseases and physical impairments, she dared to hope the same for herself. Her belief in Jesus' power made her bold—she was determined to reach out to him for help. But because she was legally unclean and embarrassed by her illness, she wanted to slip through the crowd and touch his robe without attracting any attention. Just coming in contact with the fringe or hem of Jesus' garment—a detail Matthew and Luke tell us (Matthew 9:20;

Luke 8:44)—would be enough to heal her, she reasoned with amazing faith.

Later in Mark's Gospel, we read that "wherever Jesus came, in villages, cities, or country, they laid the sick in the market places, and besought him that they might touch even the fringe of his garment; and as many as touched it were made well" (Mark 6:56; see also Matthew 14:35-36). It is likely that Jesus, a pious Jew, wore tassels called *tzitzi* attached to the corners of his robe or cloak, as enjoined by the law: "The LORD said to Moses: '. . . Bid [the people of Israel] to make tassels on the corners of their garments throughout the generations, and to put upon the tassel of each corner a cord of blue; and it shall be to you a tassel to look upon and remember all the commandments of the LORD' " (Numbers 15:37-39; see also Deuteronomy 22:12). Consequently, the popular belief that such tassels had the power to heal or bring good fortune, especially when worn by holy men, may have influenced this woman's thinking.

The woman's hemorrhage ceased when she touched Jesus' clothing, and she immediately felt that she had been healed (Mark 5:29). She had come up behind Jesus, unseen by him as she stretched her hand out to his robe (5:27). Now her hope had been fulfilled—after so many years of suffering, she was well, her body healthy and free of pain! But when she tried to disappear into the noisy throng unnoticed, Jesus gave her away.

Jesus was certain that he had not simply

been jostled accidentally in the press of the crowd. He'd been touched purposefully by a hand reaching out in eager faith, and he felt energy go out from him (Mark 5:30). When Jesus asked, "Who touched me?" (5:31), he wanted to know who had drawn upon his power with such firm confidence in him.

The woman must have trembled, ashamed to admit that in her uncleanness she had dared to touch the teacher. Yet she was sure of his mercy, for had he not just granted her healing? So, falling at his feet, she told "the whole truth" (Mark 5:33). Her story, so long one of repeated disappointments, had culminated in joy and gratitude. She "declared in the presence of all the people why she had touched him, and how she had been immediately healed" (Luke 8:47). In reply, Jesus commended and affirmed her: "Daughter, your faith has made you well; go in peace, and be healed of your disease" (Mark 5:34).

In summing up the significance of this woman's encounter with Jesus, biblical scholar George Montague, S.M., noted that the account has much to teach us:

First, healing is a personal encounter with Jesus. It is not a magical or mechanical event, though physical touch may be involved. The healed person must meet Jesus, even if the meeting takes place after the healing. Second, a public confession of Jesus is part of the healing process. Others may thus come to faith through this woman's witness. Finally, even though the physical event of her healing has taken place already, Jesus' word of healing completes the action. He further personalizes it, and teaches that her touch would have been meaningless without faith. (*Mark: Good News for Hard Times*)

Not only did Jesus restore this woman's health, he also restored her place in society. When Jesus called the woman forth from the crowd to publicly acknowledge her healing, he established her as clean in the eyes of all. By Jesus' gracious affirmation of her, she was given full and abundant life.

Pondering the Word

1. List all the verbs in this story that describe what the woman with the hemorrhage did and what she experienced. What do they indicate about this woman's character?

_____

_____

_____

_____

_____

_____

_____

_____

2. What does Mark's account reveal about Jesus? How would you characterize Jesus' response to this woman? What does this suggest to you about how he regarded and treated all women?

_____

_____

_____

_____

_____

_____

_____

_____

_____

3. Why do you think Jesus wanted to know who touched him?

_____

_____

_____

_____

_____

_____

_____

_____

_____

4. Reflect on these other instances in the gospels in which Jesus said, "Your faith has made you well": Luke 7:36-50; Mark 10:46-52; Luke 17:11-19. What do these scenes indicate about the importance of faith? How did those in need respond to Jesus?

_____

_____

_____

_____

_____

_____

_____

_____

_____

_____

5. Jesus told the woman whom he healed, "Go in peace" (Mark 5:34). In what ways do you think she experienced peace because of this healing? Describe how you think her life changed after she was freed of her long-standing and troubling condition.

_____

_____

_____

_____

_____

_____

_____

_____

6. Read Mark 5:21-24, 35-43, the account about Jairus and his daughter. What similarities do you see in this story and in that about the woman with the hemorrhage?

_____

_____

_____

_____

_____

_____

_____

_____

Living the Word

1. Imagine yourself in this scene with Jesus. What is the one pressing need you would bring to him? How do you imagine him responding to you?

_____

_____

_____

_____

_____

_____

_____

_____

_____

_____

2. In what ways do you identify with the woman in Mark 5:24-34? Do you have a need that is so long-standing—like the woman's twelve-year problem—that you feel discouraged and have little hope of any solution? How does this gospel story give you hope?

_____

_____

_____

_____

_____

_____

_____

_____

_____

_____

3. What are some concrete ways that you can reach out and "touch" the garment of Jesus? Are you willing to take a risk, like this woman did, to try something new (perhaps fasting, asking others to pray with you, attending a healing Mass, or receiving the Sacrament of the Anointing of the Sick)?

_____

_____

_____

_____

_____

_____

_____

_____

4. When have you felt Jesus' power healing you physically or spiritually? What was your reaction to this healing? How did it change your life?

_____

_____

_____

_____

_____

_____

_____

_____

5. Can you think of any situation when you felt that Jesus honored or commended you for putting faith in him? How did you respond?

_____

_____

_____

_____

_____

_____

_____

_____

_____

6. Do you know someone with a chronic illness? What might you do to show them love and compassion?

_____

_____

_____

_____

_____

_____

_____

_____

_____

_____

Rooted in the Word

The Woman with the Hemorrhage:
A Portrait of Faith

The woman who suffered from the bleeding disorder for so many years heard the reports of those who had been healed by Jesus (Mark 5:27), believed them, and cast herself upon his mercy. Faith in Jesus' compassion and power gave her the courage to approach him with the confident expectation that she would be healed simply by touching his garments.

Sixteen centuries later the great Carmelite reformer St. Teresa of Avila mirrored the faith of this woman of the gospels when she wrote, "God is full of compassion and never fails those who are afflicted and despised, if they trust in him alone." Writing in a very similar vein, St. Jane de Chantal, founder of the Congregation of the Visitation, encouraged her sisters, "With the confidence of a son, rest in the care and love that divine Providence has for you in all your needs. Look upon Providence as a child does its mother who loves him tenderly. You can be sure that God loves you incomparably more."

"Now faith is the assurance of things hoped for, the conviction of things not seen," the author of Hebrews wrote (11:1). He then described the faith of Noah, Abraham, Moses, and other heroes. We can add to that list the faith of those in the gospels—like the woman with the hemorrhage, Jairus, the centurion of Capernaum, and Bartimaeus—and the many holy men and women throughout the history of the church, who make up the "great cloud of witnesses" that surrounds us (12:1).

Read and prayerfully reflect on these additional Scripture passages that illustrate faith and its fruits and teach us how to grow in faith:

They brought the boy to [Jesus]; and when the spirit saw him, immediately it convulsed the boy, and he fell on the ground and rolled about, foaming at the mouth. And Jesus asked his father, "How long has he had this?" And he said, "From childhood. And it has often cast him into the fire and into the water, to destroy him; but if you can do anything, have pity on us and help us." And Jesus said to him, "If you can! All things are possible to him who believes." Immediately the father of the child cried out and said, "I believe; help my unbelief!" And when Jesus saw that a crowd came running together, he rebuked the unclean spirit, saying to it, "You dumb and deaf spirit, I command you, come out of him, and never enter him again." And after crying out and convulsing him terribly, it came out, and the boy was like a corpse; so that most of them said, "He is dead." But Jesus took him by the hand and lifted him up, and he arose. (Mark 9:20-27)

Jesus answered [his disciples], "Have faith in God. Truly, I say to you, whoever says to this mountain, 'Be taken up and cast into the sea,' and does not doubt in his heart, but believes that what he says will come to pass, it will be done for him. Therefore I tell you, whatever you ask in prayer, believe that you have received it, and it will be yours." (Mark 11:22-24)

The apostles said to the Lord, "Increase our faith!" And the Lord said, "If you had faith as a grain of mustard seed, you could say to this sycamine tree, 'Be rooted up, and planted in the sea,' and it would obey you." (Luke 17:5-6)

In hope [Abraham] believed against hope, that he should become the father of many nations; as he had been told, "So shall your descendants be." He did not weaken in faith when he considered his own body, which was as good as dead because he was about a hundred years old, or when he considered the barrenness of Sarah's womb. No distrust made him waver concerning the promise of God, but he grew strong in his faith as he gave glory to God, fully convinced that God was able to do what he had promised. (Romans 4:18-21)

You know that the testing of your faith produces steadfastness. And let steadfastness have its full effect, that you may be perfect and complete, lacking in nothing. (James 1:3-4)

As the outcome of your faith you obtain the salvation of your souls. (1 Peter 1:9)

Treasuring the Word

A Reading from *Women of the Bible* by Ann Spangler and Jean E. Syswerda

The Woman with the Issue of Blood

The woman hovered at the edge of the crowd. Nobody watched as she melted into the throng of bodies—just one more bee entering the hive. Her shame faded, quickly replaced by a rush of relief. No one had prevented her from joining in. No one had recoiled at her touch.

She pressed closer, but a noisy swarm of men still blocked her view. She could hear Jairus, a ruler of the synagogue, raising his voice above the others, pleading with Jesus to come and heal his daughter before it was too late.

Suddenly the group in front of her shifted, parting like the waters of the Jordan before the children of the promise. It was all she needed. Her arm darted through the opening, fingers brushing the hem of his garment. Instantly, she felt a warmth spread through her, flushing out the pain, clearing out the decay. Her skin prickled and shivered. She felt strong and able, like a young girl coming into her own—so glad and giddy, in fact, that her feet wanted to rush her away before she created a spectacle by laughing out loud at her quiet miracle.

But Jesus blocked her escape and silenced the crowd with a curious question: "Who touched me?"

"Who touched him? He must be joking!" voices murmured. "People are pushing and shoving just to get near him!"

Shaking now, the woman fell at his feet: "For twelve years, I have been hemorrhaging internally and have spent all my money on doctors but only grown worse. Today, I knew that if I could just touch your garment, I would be healed." But touching, she knew, meant spreading her defilement—even to the rabbi.

Twelve years of loneliness. Twelve years in which physicians had bled her of all her wealth. Her private affliction becoming a matter of public record. Every cup she handled, every chair she sat on could transmit defilement to others. Even though her impurity was considered a ritual matter rather than an ethical one, it had rendered her an outcast, making it impossible for her to live with a husband, bear a child, or enjoy the intimacy of friends and family. Surely the rabbi would censure her.

But instead of scolding and shaming her, Jesus praised her: "Daughter, your faith has healed you. Go in peace and be freed from your suffering."

His words must have been like water breaching a dam, breaking through her isolation, setting her free. He had addressed her not harshly, but tenderly; not as "woman" or "sinner," but rather as *daughter*.

She was no longer alone, but part of his family by virtue of her faith.

That day, countless men and women had brushed against Jesus, but only one had truly touched him. And instead of being defiled by contact with her, his own touch had proven the more contagious, rendering her pure and whole again.

Zacchaeus

Zacchaeus, make haste and come down; for I must stay at your house today.
Luke 19:5

Of all people to choose from, [Christ] singled out the chief of the tax collectors. Who can lose hope for themselves when even such a man attained salvation?
St. Ambrose, *Commentary on St. Luke's Gospel*

Zacchaeus' Tall Tale

Until Zacchaeus was visited so long ago
by saving grace in Jericho,
he'd known no joy nor satisfaction
in all that he'd possessed or wrongly gained.
Instead, he'd yearned for something he could not attain:
The sight of you, O Lord, eluded him,
for he was small of stature (and of heart).

But throwing off his dignity and pride,
he climbed the sycamore—
and grew taller than he'd ever been before.
And from this new height,
he won his first glimpse of you.

Passing by that blessed tree,
you probed its leafy shelter with keen eyes;
and catching sight of the chief of tax collectors
perched (as if awaiting fate—or was it grace he hoped to meet there?)
so precariously in his post,
you stripped bare his soul
and looked into his longing.
Then suddenly sure with knowledge of his need,
you offered yourself to him as guest:

Zacchaeus, make haste and come down;
for I must stay at your house today.

Honored by such favor and request,
gladly did Zacchaeus descend
to be host and welcome you into his home and heart.
And as that humbled heart swelled great with generosity

in gratitude that you'd so gifted him with grace,
more gladly still did he give half his goods away
and repay fourfold his failings.
Yet far greater was the recompense that he received:
Since salvation came that happy day to him and all his house,
the little man's no longer stunted by his greed and ill-gotten gains.
Growing to full stature in you, O Lord,
Zacchaeus now stands straight and tall.

Luke 19:1-10 *The Scene*

^{19:1} [Jesus] entered Jericho and was passing through. ² And there was a man named Zacchaeus; he was a chief tax collector, and rich. ³ And he sought to see who Jesus was, but could not, on account of the crowd, because he was small of stature. ⁴ So he ran on ahead and climbed up into a sycamore tree to see him, for he was to pass that way. ⁵ And when Jesus came to the place, he looked up and said to him, "Zacchaeus, make haste and come down; for I must stay at your house today." ⁶ So he made haste and came down, and received him joyfully. ⁷ And when they saw it they all murmured, "He has gone in to be the guest of a man who is a sinner." ⁸ And Zacchaeus stood and said to the Lord, "Behold, Lord, the half of my goods I give to the poor; and if I have defrauded any one of anything, I restore it fourfold." ⁹ And Jesus said to him, "Today salvation has come to this house, since he also is a son of Abraham. ¹⁰ For the Son of man came to seek and to save the lost."

Reflecting on the Word

When he awoke that morning, Zacchaeus could not have expected that he would entertain such an unusual guest in his home and relinquish half of his wealth—happily, at that—before the day was over! His encounter with Jesus was a surprising and life-changing one, and for years afterward, Zacchaeus—and all of Jericho with him—must have often recalled that memorable time when Jesus came to town.

Jesus, accompanied by his followers, was in Jericho on his way from Galilee to the Passover festival (and his death) in Jerusalem. Messianic fever ran high among the excited crowds who greeted him as he traveled to the holy city, attracted by his preaching and miracles. Could this be the Messiah, they wondered, come to deliver them from their Roman oppressors?

A prosperous commercial and agricultural town in Jesus' day, Jericho is located near the end of the Jordan Valley, not far from the Dead Sea. From Jericho, the road begins its steep climb to Jerusalem. As Jesus entered the town, Zacchaeus, one of the district tax collectors, was eager to catch a glimpse of him. However, since he wasn't a tall man, he couldn't see over the heads of the crowd. So, quick-thinking and resourceful—qualities that had likely served him well in his lucrative profession—Zacchaeus ran ahead along Jesus' route and climbed a tree so he could get a good view of the teacher with a reputation for such amazing deeds.

Zacchaeus didn't worry that day about how undignified he looked nor did he care about what anyone else thought of him. Clearly his sole concern was to see Jesus, but we wonder what, in particular, motivated that desire. Was it idle curiosity to get a look at a miracle worker? Or was Zacchaeus moved by a longing for something worth far more than anything his money could buy?

Called a chief tax collector by Luke, Zacchaeus may have been Rome's "IRS supervisor" for the whole district, with other tax agents under him (Luke 19:2). Rights to collect public revenues within the provinces of the Roman Empire were auctioned off in Rome to financial companies. Frequently the bidder who won a contract then sold rights to collect taxes in various regions to smaller speculators, who often abused their positions by charging exorbitantly high rates. Consequently, tax collectors were unpopular. The Jews of Jericho would have especially despised Zacchaeus (Luke 19:7) because his job brought him into contact with "unclean" Gentiles and probably also required that he work on the sabbath. Moreover, he not only collected the taxes demanded by the Roman occupiers but defrauded his fellow townsmen to pad his own pocket (19:8).

Zacchaeus had shrewdly accumulated his wealth and enjoyed the material comforts it brought him. Was he, nonetheless, dissatisfied with his life? If he didn't care how foolish he appeared by climbing a tree to see Jesus, perhaps he was actually hoping for a personal encounter with this preacher whose words were known to cut to the heart.

Jesus' timing is perfect: He knows just the right hour to reach a heart that is longing for him. So he took the initiative, calling out: "Zacchaeus, make haste and come down; for I must stay at your house today" (Luke 19:5). When Jesus found this strange little man sitting up in a tree, he was like a shepherd searching for his wayward sheep. Just a short time before, Jesus had told this parable to the Pharisees who objected to his association with tax collectors and sinners (Luke 15:1-2):

What man of you, having a hundred sheep, if he has lost one of them, does not leave the ninety-nine in the wilderness, and go after the one which is lost, until he finds it? And when he has found it, he lays it on his shoulders, rejoicing. And when he comes home, he calls together his friends and his neighbors, saying to them, "Rejoice with me, for I have found my sheep which was lost." (Luke 15:3-6)

In seeking out Zacchaeus, Jesus was also fulfilling God's own description of himself as Israel's "shepherd":

Behold, I, I myself will search for my sheep, and will seek them out. As a shepherd seeks out his flock when some

of his sheep have been scattered abroad, so will I seek out my sheep; and I will rescue them from all places where they have been scattered on a day of clouds and thick darkness. . . . I will seek the lost, and I will bring back the strayed, and I will bind up the crippled, and I will strengthen the weak, and the fat and the strong I will watch over; I will feed them in justice. (Ezekiel 34:11-12, 16)

Jesus called out to Zacchaeus by name, just as a shepherd "calls his own sheep by name" (John 10:3). Had he heard the crowds shouting at the little man, mocking him as he sat so oddly perched in the sycamore? Or did Jesus know Zacchaeus and his name by divine insight, just as he had "known" Nathaniel sitting under the fig tree (1:47-48)? And Zacchaeus, like the sheep, recognized the voice of the shepherd (10:4).

Zacchaeus had climbed the tree and risked his reputation to see Jesus but, paradoxically, it was Jesus who sought out Zacchaeus. Jesus' desire to be a guest in the tax collector's home—"I must stay at your house today" (Luke 19:5)—reminds us of his invitation to all: "I stand at the door and knock; if any one hears my voice and opens the door, I will come in to him and eat with him, and he with me" (Revelation 3:20).

Jesus didn't confront Zacchaeus about his sins or ask him for an account of his shady business practices. Instead, he honored

Zacchaeus with a request to be his guest. Touched by Jesus' graciousness, the little tax collector acted quickly and decisively: He "made haste and came down"—no holding back on his part or wasting time!—"and received him joyfully" (Luke 19:6). Recognizing some special quality about this itinerant rabbi, Zacchaeus immediately brought him home. And with that spontaneous, eager response to Jesus, his life was radically transformed.

When the crowds grumbled that Jesus was entering the house of a sinner, was Zacchaeus embarrassed for the Lord's sake? Perhaps he was ashamed and convicted that he was unworthy to receive this thoroughly good man who offered him his friendship. In any case, Zaccaheus was deeply moved by the Lord's presence in his home and reformed his ways.

Zacchaeus not only publicly admitted his wrongdoing to his unexpected guest but also made his repentance concrete: He spontaneously announced that he would share half of his possessions with the poor and generously repay all those whom he had defrauded (Luke 19:8). In making fourfold restitution, Zacchaeus went far beyond the requirements of the Mosaic law regarding compensation for stolen goods (Leviticus 6:1-5; Numbers 5:5-7).

Affirming Zacchaeus' repentance, Jesus declared: "Today salvation has come to this house" (Luke 19:9). Was there a surprised Mrs. Zacchaeus on the scene, and some startled children and house servants, too? Surely all the members of the household would have shared in the grace and blessings of Zacchaeus' transformation, just as Cornelius' entire household received salvation at his conversion (Acts 10:2; 11:14).

As Jesus carried out his mission "to seek and to save the lost" (Luke 19:10), tax collectors and sinners were certainly among those whom he welcomed into his kingdom (Matthew 9:10-13; 21:31-32).

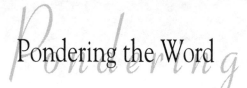

Pondering the Word

1. What might you surmise about Zacchaeus' personal character before his encounter with Jesus, considering his job as a tax collector? How do you think he might have related to his fellow Jews? To his Roman employers?

_____

_____

_____

_____

_____

_____

_____

_____

_____

2. What is the significance of Jesus addressing Zacchaeus by name before the tax collector had actually been introduced to him? Reflect on Isaiah 43:1 and Psalm 139:13-16 as you consider your answer to this question. What other gospel scenes can you think of in which Jesus called someone by name? How did they respond?

_____

_____

_____

_____

_____

_____

_____

_____

3. What similarities do you see between Zacchaeus, the tax collector-turned-apostle Matthew (Matthew 9:9-13; Mark 2:13-17; and Luke 5:27-32), and the publican in Jesus' parable in Luke 18:9-14? How were they different from one another?

_____

_____

_____

_____

_____

_____

_____

_____

4. The story of Zacchaeus' conversion comes soon after Luke's account in the previous chapter of the rich young man who was unwilling to give up his wealth to follow Jesus (Luke 18:18-23; see also Matthew 19:16-22). What do the contrasting ways in which the two responded to Jesus suggest to you about discipleship? About material possessions? About repentance?

_____

_____

_____

_____

_____

_____

_____

5. Why did Jesus call Zacchaeus a "son of Abraham" (Luke 19:9)? Read Genesis 15:5-6, Isaiah 51:2, John 8:39-40, and Romans 4:1-3, 12 to help you answer this question.

_____

_____

_____

_____

_____

_____

_____

_____

_____

6. Why do you think many Scripture scholars have called Luke's narrative about Zacchaeus a concise summary of the Christian gospel or a "mini-gospel"?

_____

_____

_____

_____

_____

_____

_____

_____

_____

_____

_____

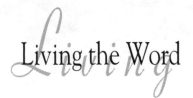

Living the Word

1. What obstacles stand in the way of your seeing Jesus clearly? What can you do to remove these obstacles and gain a better view and understanding of him?

_____

_____

_____

_____

_____

_____

_____

_____

_____

2. Do you occasionally hesitate to respond to Jesus because you feel self-conscious or worried about what others might think of you? Or because you are afraid that your response might cost you a great price? How can you overcome these fears?

_____

_____

_____

_____

_____

_____

_____

_____

_____

3. Do you think of everything that you have—your talents, your money, your time—as belonging to God? How generous are you with the resources and gifts God has given you? In what ways do you share them with others?

4. Zacchaeus expressed his repentance concretely. Ask the Holy Spirit to show you what specific actions you should take to respond fully to Jesus' offer of salvation. Write a brief prayer asking Jesus for his help to do this.

5. Jesus came to "seek and to save the lost" (Luke 19:10) and ate with sinners (19:7). How do you treat or react to people who are on the margins of society?

_____

_____

_____

_____

_____

_____

_____

_____

_____

6. How has your relationship with Jesus affected your "household"—your family, friends, coworkers, and neighbors? Does Zacchaeus' conversion give you hope for anyone dear to you who is distant from the Lord? Does it give you hope that your own life can be transformed by a deeper personal encounter with the Lord?

_____

_____

_____

_____

_____

_____

_____

_____

_____

Rooted in the Word

Zacchaeus: A Portrait of a Repentant Heart

When Zacchaeus discovers that he is personally loved by the one who introduces himself as the awaited Messiah," noted Pope John Paul II in one of his homilies, "he is touched to the depth of his soul and opens his heart." Zacchaeus experienced a profound conversion of heart in his encounter with Jesus.

Conversion is a work of the grace of God, who gives us strength to begin anew. "It is in discovering the greatness of God's love that our heart is shaken by the horror and weight of sin and begins to fear offending God by sin and being separated from him. The human heart is converted by looking upon him whom our sins have pierced" (*Catechism of the Catholic Church*, 1432). Zacchaeus' conversion of heart led him to repent of his sinful practices—and his repentance showed itself to be genuine as he mended his ways in a true conversion of life.

Repentance is the path back to God when we've gotten off track or fallen from his ways. When we repent, we make an about-face, acknowledging and turning away from our sins and wrongdoing and turning toward God. As the *Catechism* further explains, "Interior repentance is a radical reorientation of our whole life, a return, a conversion to God with all our heart, an end of sin, a turn-ing away from evil, with repugnance toward the evil actions we have committed. At the same time it entails the desire and resolution to change one's life, with hope of God's mercy and trust in the help of his grace" (1431).

Read and prayerfully reflect on these additional Scripture passages about repentance and its fruits as well as about God's love for repentant sinners:

> Have mercy on me, O God,
>   according to thy steadfast love;
>   according to thy abundant mercy
>   blot out my transgressions.
> Wash me thoroughly from my iniquity,
>   and cleanse me from my sin!
> Hide thy face from my sins,
>   and blot out all my iniquities.
> Create in me a clean heart, O God,
>   and put a new and right spirit
>   within me.
> Cast me not away from thy presence,
>   and take not thy holy Spirit from me.
> Restore to me the joy of thy salvation,
>   and uphold me with a willing spirit.
>   (Psalm 51:1-2, 9-12)

As [Jesus] sat at table in his house, many tax collectors and sinners were sitting with Jesus and his disciples; for there were many who followed him. And the scribes of the Pharisees, when they saw that he was eating with sinners and tax collectors, said to his disciples, "Why does he eat with tax collectors and sinners?" And when Jesus heard it, he said to them, "Those who are well have no need of a physician, but those who are sick; I came not to call the righteous, but sinners." (Mark 2:15-17)

[Jesus said to him:] "Simon, I have something to say to you." And he answered, "What is it, Teacher?" "A certain creditor had two debtors; one owed five hundred denarii, and the other fifty. When they could not pay, he forgave them both. Now which of them will love him more?" Simon answered, "The one, I suppose, to whom he forgave more." And he said to him, "You have judged rightly." Then turning toward the woman he said to Simon, "Do you see this woman? I entered your house, you gave me no water for my feet, but she has wet my feet with her tears and wiped them with her hair. You gave me no kiss, but from the time I came in she has not ceased to kiss my feet. You did not anoint my head with oil, but she has anointed my feet with ointment. Therefore I tell you, her sins, which are many, are forgiven, for she loved much; but he who is forgiven little, loves little." And he said to her, "Your sins are forgiven." Then those who were at table with him began to say among themselves, "Who is this, who even forgives sins?" (Luke 7:40-49)

The Lord is . . . forbearing toward you, not wishing that any should perish, but that all should reach repentance. (2 Peter 3:9)

If we confess our sins, he is faithful and just, and will forgive our sins and cleanse us from all unrighteousness. (1 John 1:9)

Treasuring the Word

A Reading from Pope John Paul II's *Letter to Priests for Holy Thursday 2002*

Zacchaeus: A Biblical Icon of the Sacrament of Mercy

In order to bring out certain specific aspects of the unique saving dialogue that is sacramental confession, I would like to use the "biblical icon" of the meeting between Jesus and Zacchaeus. To me it seems that what takes place between Jesus and the "chief tax collector" of Jericho resembles in a number of ways the celebration of the sacrament of mercy. . . .

The story . . . presents the meeting between Jesus and Zacchaeus as if it happened by chance. Jesus enters Jericho and moves through the city accompanied by the crowd (Luke 19:3). In climbing the sycamore tree, Zacchaeus seems prompted by curiosity alone. At times, God's meetings with man do appear to be merely fortuitous. But nothing that God does happens by chance. . . . This is precisely the case of Zacchaeus. Everything that happens to him is amazing. If there had not been, at a certain point, the "surprise" of Christ looking up at him, perhaps he would have remained a silent spectator of the Lord moving through the streets of Jericho.

Jesus would have passed *by*, not *into*, his life. Zacchaeus had no idea that the curiosity which had prompted him to do such an unusual thing was already the fruit of a mercy which had preceded him, attracted him and was about to change him in the depths of his heart.

. . . "When Jesus came to the place, he looked up and said to him, 'Zacchaeus, make haste and come down; for I must stay at your house today' " (Luke 19:5). Every encounter with someone wanting to go to confession, even when the request is somewhat superficial because it is poorly motivated and prepared, can become, through the surprising grace of God, that "place" near the sycamore tree where Christ looked up at Zacchaeus. How deeply Christ's gaze penetrated the Jericho publican's soul is impossible for us to judge. But we do know that that same gaze looks upon each of our penitents. . . . For Zacchaeus, it must have been a stunning experience to hear himself called by his name, a name which many of his townsmen spoke with contempt. Now he hears it spoken in a tone of tenderness, expressing not just trust but familiarity, insistent friendship. Yes,

Jesus speaks to Zacchaeus like an old friend, forgotten maybe, but a friend who has nonetheless remained faithful, and who enters with the gentle force of affection into the life and into the home of his re-discovered friend: "Make haste and come down; for I must stay at your house today."

Luke's account is remarkable for the tone of the language: everything is so personal, so tactful, so affectionate! Not only is the text filled with humanity; it suggests insistence, an urgency to which Jesus gives voice as the one offering the definitive revelation of God's mercy. He says: "I must stay at your house", or to translate even more literally: "I need to stay at your house." Following the mysterious road map which the Father has laid out for him, Jesus runs into Zacchaeus along the way. He pauses near him as if the meeting had been planned from the beginning. Despite all the murmuring of human malice, the home of this sinner is about to become a place of revelation, the scene of a miracle of mercy. True, this will not happen if Zacchaeus does not free his heart from the ligatures of egoism and from his unjust and fraudulent ways. But mercy has already

come to him as a gratuitous and overflowing gift. Mercy has preceded him!

This is what happens in every sacramental encounter. We must not think that it is the sinner, through his own independent journey of conversion, who earns mercy. On the contrary, it is mercy that impels him along the path of conversion. Left to himself, man can do nothing and he deserves nothing. Before being man's journey to God, confession is God's arrival at a person's home. . . .

. . . In the sacrament, the penitent first meets not "the commandments of God" but, in Jesus, "the God of the commandments." To Zacchaeus, Jesus offers himself: "I must stay at your house." He himself is the gift that awaits Zacchaeus, and he is also "God's law" for Zacchaeus. When we see our encounter with Jesus as a gift, even the most demanding features of the law assume the "lightness" of grace, in line with that supernatural dynamic which prompted Saint Paul to say: "If you are led by the Spirit, you are not under the law" (Galatians 5:18). Every celebration of Penance should cause the soul of the penitent to leap with the same joy that Christ's words inspired in Zacchaeus, who "made haste and came down and received him joyfully" (Luke 19:6).

Bartimaeus

Master, let me receive my sight.
Mark 10:51

Let us imitate [Bartimaeus]. Even if God does not give us immediately what we ask, even if many people try to put us off our prayers, let us still go on praying.
St. John Chrysostom, *Homilies on St. Matthew,* 66

The Radiance of Faith

How long since he had
last seen the shining sun
whose light now played across his face
as he dozed in its comforting warmth?

How long since he had
marveled at the sight of the brilliant bougainvillea
that lined the road outside Jericho
where he sat each day begging?

Bartimaeus could not remember,
for his life now seemed to him
an endless night
in which he blindly strained to pierce
the black shroud imprisoning him in darkness.
Yet in this deep gloom,
he still dreamed
of a new dawn to fill his sightless eyes.

Then suddenly his slumbering hopes awoke:
Of late the beggar had heard of strange happenings in Galilee—
and now the wonder-working rabbi from Nazareth
was passing right in front of him
as he walked the road toward Jerusalem!

Jesus, Son of David, have mercy on me!

Bartimaeus' cry was full of faith.
Blind though he was, his heart was unerring
as he perceived that light was close at hand
(and kindness too).

Master, let me receive my sight.

Who can open the eyes of the blind?
Yet the beggar was bold to ask not for money
but for mercy and for miracle.

And in return for faith's audacity,
the word was spoken and grace bestowed:

Go your way. Your faith has made you well.

Was the master's face
(smiling his delight in the giving of this gift)
the first that Bartimaeus saw,
bright recompense for the pains of blindness
so long borne?

Eyes and heart now aglow
with new light and the radiance of faith,
Bartimaeus followed Jesus on his way,
not wanting to lose sight
of him who forever shatters all our darkness.

10:46 They came to Jericho; and as he was leaving Jericho with his disciples and a great multitude, Bartimaeus, a blind beggar, the son of Timaeus, was sitting by the roadside. 47 And when he heard that it was Jesus of Nazareth, he began to cry out and say, "Jesus, Son of David, have mercy on me!" 48 And many rebuked him, telling him to be silent; but he cried out all the more, "Son of David, have mercy on me!" 49 And Jesus stopped and said, "Call him." And they called the blind man, saying to him, "Take heart; rise, he is calling you." 50 And throwing off his mantle he sprang up and came to Jesus. 51 And Jesus said to him, "What do you want me to do for you?" And the blind man said to him, "Master, let me receive my sight." 52 And Jesus said to him, "Go your way; your faith has made you well." And immediately he received his sight and followed him on the way.

See also Matthew 20:29-34;
Luke 18:35-43

Reflecting on the Word

Jesus was quite busy while he was in Jericho. His lively exchange with the blind beggar, Bartimaeus, occurred during his same visit there as the extraordinary meal with Zacchaeus. Mark noted that Bartimaeus encountered Jesus as he was leaving the town, while Luke placed the incident—though without naming the blind man—as Jesus drew near to it (Luke 18:35).

Jesus had set out from Galilee to celebrate the Passover in Jerusalem, and his road ran directly through Jericho, which lies eighteen miles northeast of the holy city. His disciples and a growing band of pilgrims accompanied him, yet as the company approached the place where the Passover lamb was to be sacrificed, none recognized Jesus' true identity and his paschal destiny awaiting him there.

Enthusiastic crowds greeted Jesus along his way, buoyed by the hope that he was the Messiah who would restore Israel. Bartimaeus heard their cheers. Like his fellow townsman Zacchaeus, the blind beggar wasn't concerned about what others would think of his forward behavior. In his desire to gain the attention of the miracle worker whom he had heard so much about, he began to cry out loudly as Jesus neared the stretch of road where he sat begging for alms.

Bartimaeus is the first in Mark's Gospel to address Jesus as the "Son of David" (Mark 10:47), a messianic title given to the heir of the promise made to David through Nathan (see 2 Samuel 7:12-16; Psalm 89:3-4, 29,

35-36). As Scripture scholar Philip Van Linden has observed, "The title he gives Jesus, 'Son of David,' indicates that he, a *blind* beggar, actually *sees who Jesus is* more clearly than the disciples and crowd who have been with him all along!" Bartimaeus' use of this title also prepares Mark's readers to recognize Jesus as the long-awaited Messiah.

Determined to be heard, Bartimaeus called out persistently, raising his voice above the noise of the crowds. Bystanders were annoyed by his shouting—perhaps because his cries were drowning out the rabbi's teaching—and tried to silence him. Undaunted, he ignored their rebukes. This was a once-in-a-lifetime opportunity that the blind beggar didn't want to miss. And Jesus heard his cry!

Once again Jesus was attentive to the longings of someone who was not ashamed to reveal his heart so publicly. He summoned Bartimaeus. The bystanders who earlier had been so irritated recognized the compassion in Jesus' voice and now encouraged the blind man: "Take heart; rise, he is calling you" (Mark 10:49). Long accustomed to begging for alms, this time Bartimaeus wanted much more than a few coins and boldly asked Jesus to restore his sight.

Bartimaeus didn't hesitate to seize the moment. Faith and desire propelled him forward. Even in his blindness, he knew which direction to turn for help. He sprang up eagerly, throwing off his cloak as he responded to Jesus' call. St. Josemaría Escrivá reflected insightfully on Bartimaeus' action:

> He threw off his mantle! I don't know if you have ever lived through a war, but many years ago I had occasion to visit a battlefield shortly after an engagement. There, strewn all over the ground, were greatcoats, water bottles, haversacks stuffed with family souvenirs, letters, photographs of loved ones . . . which belonged, moreover, not to the vanquished but to the victors! All these items had become superfluous in the bid to race forward and leap over the enemy defenses. Just as happened to Bartimaeus, as he raced towards Christ. (*Friends of God*)

Bartimaeus didn't want to be hindered in any way as he leapt up toward Jesus, so he cast aside his cloak. The garment had provided warmth, protection, and security. Perhaps he had also used it to collect the coins tossed to him as he begged. But now Bartimaeus was free and unhampered. Earlier in his Gospel, Mark had recorded Jesus' teaching: "No one sews a piece of unshrunk cloth on an old garment; if he does, the patch tears away from it, the new from the old, and a worse tear is made" (Mark 2:21). Seen in this light, Bartimaeus casting off his mantel can be understood as a symbol of him leaving behind the "old order" and embracing a new way of life.

"Master, let me receive my sight" (Mark 10:51). Bartimaeus' original Aramaic form of address was more solemn than the usual English translation of "master" or "rabbi" implies. It was often used when speaking to God. In the New Testament, the only ones who addressed Jesus in this way were Bartimaeus and Mary Magdalene as she cried out to the risen Lord near the empty tomb (John 20:16).

Jesus commended Bartimaeus' faith in his healing power. With deep spiritual insight, the blind beggar had perceived who Jesus was and what he was capable of doing. Jesus then honored his request and restored his physical sight. Most likely the crowd recognized the enormous significance of the healing: The eyes of the blind were opened exactly as the messianic prophecies foretold (see Isaiah 35:5). When Jesus began his ministry, he had visited the synagogue in Nazareth and read from the Book of Isaiah, declaring to his listeners that the prophet's words were being fulfilled:

> The Spirit of the Lord is upon me,
> because he has anointed me to preach good news to the poor.
> He has sent me to proclaim release to the captives
> and recovering of sight to the blind,
> to set at liberty those who are oppressed,
> to proclaim the acceptable year of the Lord.
> (Luke 4:18-19; see also Isaiah 61:1-2)

84

Grateful for Jesus' mercy and for his new ability to see, Bartimaeus immediately "followed [Jesus] on the way" (Mark 10:52). With this simple phrase, Mark calls to mind what it means to be a disciple: one who willingly follows the master, sharing in his life and mission. "If any man would come after me," Jesus had told his disciples even as he announced to them his coming Passion, "let him deny himself and take up his cross and follow me. For whoever would save his life will lose it; and whoever loses his life for my sake and the gospel will save it" (Mark 8:34-36).

Not wanting to lose sight so soon of the one who had given him new vision, Bartimaeus joined those who were going to the Passover festival with the master. But none in this company of Jesus' followers realized that the road up to Jerusalem would also lead to Golgotha.

In Luke's account of this healing, he adds that the man who received his sight "followed [Jesus], glorifying God; and all the people, when they saw it, gave praise to God" (Luke 18:43). Faith opened the way for the healing power of God in Bartimaeus' life, and all who witnessed the effects of this power at work gave God glory and praise.

Pondering the Word

1. Bartimaeus asked Jesus to have mercy on him (Mark 10:47-48). How would you define the word "mercy"? Read Psalm 51:1, Psalm 103:4, Luke 6:36, and Ephesians 2:4-7 for insight into God's mercy.

_____

_____

_____

_____

_____

_____

_____

_____

2. Choose three adjectives that you think best describe Bartimaeus. In what ways did these traits help Bartimaeus to be healed?

_____

_____

_____

_____

_____

_____

_____

_____

3. Why do you think Jesus asked Bartimaeus, "What do you want me to do for you?" (Mark 10:51)? Compare Bartimaeus' answer with the answer that James and John gave to the same question in Mark 10:35-37.

_____

_____

_____

_____

_____

_____

_____

_____

4. Why do you think Jesus responded to Bartimaeus' cries? What does this encounter with Bartimaeus tell you about Jesus?

_____

_____

_____

_____

_____

_____

_____

_____

_____

5. Jesus accused the Pharisees of being blind (Matthew 23:16-19 and John 9:39-41). What do you think caused Jesus to make such a charge? What were the Pharisees unable to "see"?

_____

_____

_____

_____

_____

_____

_____

_____

_____

6. What might you conclude from this story about the relationship between faith and healing?

_____

_____

_____

_____

_____

_____

_____

_____

_____

_____

Living the Word

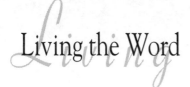

1. Bartimaeus seized the opportunity presented by his spontaneous encounter with Jesus. When have you encountered Jesus unexpectedly? What impact did this encounter have on your life?

_____

_____

_____

_____

_____

_____

_____

_____

2. Detail the various steps by which the exchange between Bartimaeus and Jesus progressed. What have you learned from this progression?

_____

_____

_____

_____

_____

_____

_____

_____

3. If Jesus were to ask you the same question right now that he asked Bartimaeus—"What do you want me to do for you?"—how would you answer?

_____

_____

_____

_____

_____

_____

_____

_____

_____

_____

4. How free and confident are you to make your requests known to the Lord? What hinders you in your response to him? How can you overcome these hindrances?

_____

_____

_____

_____

_____

_____

_____

_____

_____

_____

5. In what areas of life do you think you are spiritually blind? Can you think of any situation when you felt that God "opened your eyes" and gave you a deeper understanding of who he is?

_____

_____

_____

_____

_____

_____

_____

_____

6. Are you embarrassed by panhandlers and street people who publicly call attention to themselves and their needs? Why? How do you think Jesus would respond to them?

_____

_____

_____

_____

_____

_____

_____

_____

Rooted in the Word

Bartimaeus: A Portrait of Perseverance in Prayer

Bartimaeus was persistent in his cries to Jesus, with a perseverance animated by both need and faith. Blind, he wanted to be healed—and he had the firm conviction that Jesus had the power to grant his request:

> [Bartimaeus'] is an active faith; he shouts out, he persists, despite the people getting in his way. And he manages to get Jesus to hear him and call him. God wanted this episode to be recorded in the Gospel, to teach us how we should believe and how we should pray—with conviction, with urgency, with constancy, in spite of the obstacles, with simplicity, until we manage to get Jesus to listen to us. (*The Navarre Bible: The Gospel of St. Luke*)

In asking for healing, Bartimaeus repeatedly cried out, "Jesus, Son of David, have mercy on me!" (Mark 10:47-48). The ten lepers who asked Jesus to cleanse them (Luke 17:11-19) and the man whose son suffered from epilepsy (Matthew 17:14-21) also implored Jesus for mercy. "Lord, have mercy!" is one of the most common and heartfelt prayers of every Christian, and it has been given a prominent place in the Church's liturgical prayers.

Persistence like Bartimaeus' is seen throughout the New Testament, as in the examples of the paralytic and his friends who lowered him through the roof in order to gain access to Jesus (Luke 5:17-20) and the Canaanite woman who determinedly asked Jesus to heal her daughter (Matthew 15:22-28). We can learn from these men and women to be persevering in our prayer and not lose heart, confident that God hears and is willing to answer. As St. Thomas Aquinas explained reassuringly, "When we address a petition to God, constancy and persistence are never inexpedient. Quite the opposite. They are pleasing to God" (*Compendium of Theology*, II, 2).

Read and prayerfully reflect on these additional Scripture passages that teach us to pray with faith and perseverance:

> [Jesus said:] "Ask, and it will be given you; seek, and you will find; knock, and it will be opened to you. For every one who asks receives, and he who seeks finds, and to him who knocks it will be opened. Or what man of you, if his son asks him for bread, will give him a stone? Or if he asks for a fish, will give him a serpent? If you then, who are evil, know how to give good gifts to your children,

how much more will your Father who is in heaven give good things to those who ask him!" (Matthew 7:7-11)

[Jesus] said to them, "Which of you who has a friend will go to him at midnight and say to him, 'Friend, lend me three loaves; for a friend of mine has arrived on a journey, and I have nothing to set before him'; and he will answer from within, 'Do not bother me; the door is now shut, and my children are with me in bed; I cannot get up and give you anything'? I tell you, though he will not get up and give him anything because he is his friend, yet because of his importunity he will rise and give him whatever he needs." (Luke 11:5-8)

[Jesus] told them a parable, to the effect that they ought always to pray and not lose heart. He said, "In a certain city there was a judge who neither feared God nor regarded man; and there was a widow in that city who kept coming to

him and saying, 'Vindicate me against my adversary.' For a while he refused; but afterward he said to himself, 'Though I neither fear God nor regard man, yet because this widow bothers me, I will vindicate her, or she will wear me out by her continual coming.'" And the Lord said, "Hear what the unrighteous judge says. And will not God vindicate his elect, who cry to him day and night? Will he delay long over them? I tell you, he will vindicate them speedily. Nevertheless, when the Son of man comes, will he find faith on earth?" (Luke 18:1-8)

Pray at all times in the Spirit, with all prayer and supplication. To that end keep alert with all perseverance, making supplication for all the saints. (Ephesians 6:18)

Have no anxiety about anything, but in everything by prayer and supplication with thanksgiving let your requests be made known to God. (Philippians 4:6)

Treasuring the Word

A Reading from *Friends of God* by St. Josemaría Escrivá

The Faith of Bartimaeus

As Jesus "was leaving Jericho, with his disciples and a great multitude, Bartimaeus, the blind man, Timaeus' son, was sitting there by the wayside, begging" (Mark 10:46). Hearing the commotion the crowd was making, the blind man asked, "What is happening?" They told him, "It is Jesus of Nazareth." At this his soul was so fired with faith in Christ that he cried out, "Jesus, son of David, have pity on me" (10:47).

Don't you too feel the same urge to cry out? You who also are waiting at the side of the way, of this highway of life that is so very short? You who need more light, you who need more grace to make up your mind to seek holiness? Don't you feel an urgent need to cry out, "Jesus, son of David, have pity on me?" What a beautiful aspiration for you to repeat again and again! . . .

"Many of them rebuked him, telling him to be silent" (Mark 10:48). As people have done to you, when you sensed that Jesus was passing your way. Your heart beat faster and you too began to cry out, prompted by intimate longing. Then your friends, the need to do the done thing, the easy life, your sur-

roundings, all conspired to tell you: "Keep quiet, don't cry out. Who are you to be calling Jesus? Don't bother him."

But poor Bartimaeus would not listen to them. He cried out all the more: "Son of David, have pity on me." Our Lord, who had heard him right from the beginning, let him persevere in his prayer. He does the same with you. Jesus hears our cries from the very first, but he waits. He wants us to be convinced that we need him. He wants us to beseech him, to persist, like the blind man waiting by the road from Jericho. . . .

"And Jesus stopped and told them to call him." Some of the better people in the crowd turned to the blind man and said, "Take heart. Rise up, he is calling you" (Mark 10:49). Here you have the Christian vocation! But God does not call only once. Bear in mind that Our Lord is seeking us at every moment: get up, he tells us, put aside your indolence, your easy life, your petty selfishness, your silly little problems. Get up from the ground, where you are lying prostrate and shapeless. Acquire height, weight and volume, and a supernatural outlook.

"Whereupon the man threw away his cloak and leapt to his feet, and so came to him"

(Mark 10:50). He threw aside his cloak! . . . Never forget that Christ cannot be reached without sacrifice. We have to get rid of everything that gets in the way. . . .

And now begins a dialogue with God, a marvelous dialogue that moves us and sets our hearts on fire, for you and I are now Bartimaeus. Christ, who is God, begins to speak and asks, *Quid tibi vis faciam?* "What do you want me to do for you?" The blind man answers, "Lord, that I may see" (Mark 10:51). How utterly logical! How about yourself, can you really see? Haven't you too experienced at times what happened to the blind man of Jericho? I can never forget how, when meditating on this passage many years back, and realizing that Jesus was expecting something of me, though I myself did not know what it was, I made up my own aspirations: "Lord, what is it you want? What are you asking of me?" I had the feeling that he wanted me to take on something new and the cry *Rabboni, ut videam*, "Master, that I may see," moved me to beseech Christ again and again, "Lord, whatever it is that you wish, let it be done."

Pray with me now to Our Lord: *doce me facere voluntatem tuam, quia Deus meus us tu* (Psalm 143:10), "teach me to do your will, for you are my God." In short, our lips should express a true desire on our part to correspond effectively to our Creator's promptings, striving to follow out his plans with unshakable faith, being fully convinced that he cannot fail us. . . .

But let us go back to the scene outside Jericho. It is now to you that Christ is speaking. He asks you, "What is it you want of me?" "That I may see, Lord, that I may see." Then Jesus answers, "Away home with you. Your faith has brought you recovery. And all at once he recovered his sight and followed Jesus on his way" (Mark 10:52). Following Jesus on his way. You have understood what Our Lord was asking from you and you have decided to accompany him on his way. You are trying to walk in his footsteps, to clothe yourself in Christ's clothing, to be Christ himself: well, your faith, your faith in the light Our Lord is giving you, must be both operative and full of sacrifice. Don't fool yourself. Don't think you are going to find new ways. The faith he demands of us is as I have said. We must keep step with him, working generously and at the same time uprooting and getting rid of everything that gets in the way.

Mary of Bethany

Mary took a pound of costly ointment of pure nard and anointed the feet of Jesus and wiped his feet with her hair; and the house was filled with the fragrance of the ointment.
John 12:3

Mary illustrated the nature of love's generosity and total self-giving to another. Love does not worry much about the cost of a gift to the beloved. The gift must symbolize the total surrender of true love, regardless of the price, which may be big or small. If the price is small, but that is all one has, that is total giving. Mary focused her loving attention completely on Jesus. Her deed was simplicity itself, humble, direct, uncomplicated, selfless, loving.
Alfred McBride, O. Praem.,
The Divine Presence of Jesus

Bethany Revisited: My Love's Anointing

Mary took a pound of costly ointment of pure nard
and anointed the feet of Jesus . . .
and the house was filled with the fragrance of the ointment.

Supremely free from herself
(what enviable liberty!)
and careless of all others' thought of her
(would that I, too, lacked such inhibition
and could cease to serve my reputation),
Mary poured the costliest of gifts
upon your feet, O Lord:
a love unmeasured and full-spent,
wholly wasted for your good pleasure and praise.

Withholding nothing for herself,
generous and unreserved
she anointed those feet
(where once she sat so earnest
listening to your word)
with purest perfume,
the scent of her heart's sacrifice.

She has done a beautiful thing.

And wishing to learn from Mary's lead,
what are the spices of my life
to crush to sweet fragrance for you
for like anointing?

My hopes and dreams and disappointments;
my joys and longings and little daily delights foregone;

my fears won over and sins repented of;
my chaste fervor and innocence—

Such is my offering
distilled to perfume beyond all price,
its essence nothing but my love for you.

The Scene

Luke 10:38-42

10:38 Now as they went on their way, he entered a village; and a woman named Martha received him into her house. 39 And she had a sister called Mary, who sat at the Lord's feet and listened to his teaching. 40 But Martha was distracted with much serving; and she went to him and said, "Lord, do you not care that my sister has left me to serve alone? Tell her then to help me." 41 But the Lord answered her, "Martha, Martha, you are anxious and troubled about many things; 42 one thing is needful. Mary has chosen the good portion, which shall not be taken away from her."

The Scene

Mark 14:3-9

14:3 And while he was at Bethany in the house of Simon the leper, as he sat at table, a woman came with an alabaster jar of ointment of pure nard, very costly, and she broke the jar and poured it over his head. 4 But there were some who said to themselves indignantly, "Why was the ointment thus wasted? 5 For this ointment might have been sold for more than three hundred denarii, and given to the poor." And they reproached her. 6 But Jesus said, "Let her alone; why do you trouble her? She has done a beautiful thing to me. 7 For you always have the poor with you, and whenever you will, you can do good to them; but you will not always have me. 8 She has done what she could; she has anointed my body beforehand for burying. 9 And truly, I say to you, wherever the gospel is preached in the whole world, what she has done will be told in memory of her."

See also Matthew 26:6-13; John 12:1-8

Reflecting on the Word

She was a simple first-century woman from a negligible village in a country overshadowed by the Roman Empire, yet the memory of Mary of Bethany has endured through two millennia. Her fame is widespread, even though relatively little is known about her life. The evangelists tell nothing of her birth, family background, or social standing. However, the descriptions they so vividly paint of her encounters with Jesus give us a truer picture of her than we would gain from an entry in *Who's Who?* In each of the gospel stories about Mary of Bethany, we see her in the same place—at the Lord's feet.

The Good Portion. Martha and Mary and their brother Lazarus were dear friends of Jesus (John 11:5). Their home was a haven where he found rest and refreshment in its loving atmosphere. During the last days of his life when Jesus taught daily in the Temple, he withdrew at night to Bethany (Matthew 21:17; Mark 11:11)—most probably to the house of Martha, Mary, and Lazarus.

Hospitality is regarded very highly in the culture of the Middle East, so it's natural that Martha wanted to serve Jesus well. She loved Jesus deeply, and expressed this love concretely by preparing him a fine meal. However, Martha was an anxious, busy hostess, so occupied with cooking that she couldn't take the time to sit down with her guest. Jesus appreciated Martha's loving care, but urged her to relax and enjoy his company.

When Martha indignantly asked, "Lord, do you not care that my sister has left me to serve alone?" (Luke 10:40), she showed a self-concern that robbed her of the ability to appreciate the precious gift of the moment—fellowship with Jesus. In her complaint we find the same Greek verb, *melei*, that the disciples used in their accusation of Jesus during the storm at sea: "Do you not care if we perish?" (Mark 4:38). Jesus responded the same way to both upheavals: He calmed the troubled hearts and storms that swept around him. Jesus' gentle rebuke to Martha—"You are anxious and troubled about many things"—was meant to help her recognize how senseless and unnecessary her anxieties were. Only one thing is needed (Luke 10:41-42).

Unlike Martha, Mary was wholly present to Jesus, wholly *there* for him. She stayed near to him, not wasting any of the brief moments he spent in their house. She simply sat still at Jesus' feet and listened to his conversation. She didn't want to miss a single word he spoke. She had indeed chosen the "good portion" (Luke 10:42). Mother Basilea Schlink, founder of the Evangelical Sisterhood of Mary, described Mary well:

In Bethany Jesus found open hearts that loved him and eagerly awaited him at all times. Mary laid all else aside; it was of secondary importance to her. When Jesus came, she hastened to him and devoted herself fully to him. She was completely captivated by Jesus. She had eyes and ears for him alone, for him whom her soul loved. To love Jesus, to hear words of eternal life from his lips meant everything to her. (*The Holy Places Today*)

Mary's vision was focused on Jesus as she sat at his feet. There, so close to him, she became sensitive to what was on his heart.

We may feel sorry for Martha, left to fix the dinner alone, and resent Mary's "portion." But rather than seeing the two postures as mutually exclusive, might we not find in Martha and Mary complementary aspects of the call given to all followers of Christ? Balancing action and contemplation in a creative tension in our own lives, we dynamically express our love for Jesus through both.

The Anointing. Matthew and Mark place the anointing at a dinner held in Bethany in the home of Simon the leper, and the woman is unnamed (Matthew 26:6-7; Mark 14:3). John identifies her as Mary, and makes note of Martha's and Lazarus' presence at the meal— perhaps a celebration of Lazarus' resurrection. The fourth evangelist does not specifically say that the dinner was held in their house, but since he tells us that Martha was serving (again), we can make that assumption (John 12:1-2).

In Jesus' day, it was customary to honor guests by offering them scented water and washing their feet. Mary carried out this service with special refinement, lavishly anointing Jesus with fragrant nard. Unconcerned about what the other guests might think of her, she cared only for her master and uninhibitedly expressed her love for him.

The ointment Mary used to anoint Jesus was the aromatic essence of spikenard. The hairy stem of this small plant gives off a rich, sweet-smelling fragrance. Oil pressed from spikenard was used to make perfume, so it became an important trade item in the ancient world, transported on camelback from the Himalayan Mountains, where it grew, to merchants in the Mediterranean world. Thus, essence of spikenard was quite expensive— Mary's perfume was worth three hundred denarii. With a laborer's pay being a denarius a day at that time, it cost the equivalent of almost a year's wages. Mary's offering was indeed a generous one!

Mark adds the detail that the perfume was held in an alabaster jar (Mark 14:3). Alabaster, a fine, white or translucent variety of gypsum or calcite, is used for carving ornamental objects such as vases and flasks. Mary broke the neck of her exquisite vessel to allow the last drop of perfume to flow out. The flask was to serve no one else and no other purpose—Jesus was worthy of everything.

Mary's deed shows us some beautiful truths: Love never calculates, but wants to give the utmost. Though prudence might caution that this gesture was an extravagant waste, love obeys the promptings of the heart. A gift is truly a gift when it is accompanied by sacrifice.

All the evangelists noted that the apostles were indignant at Mary's extravagance. While their thought that the poor could have been better served by this money was well intended (Matthew 26:8-9; Mark 14:4-5; John 12:4-5), their complaint against Mary shows that they missed the point of her symbolic action. Jesus himself interpreted Mary's "beautiful" deed to them, explaining that the anointing was a preparation for his burial (Matthew 26:10, 12; Mark 14:6, 8). At Jesus' birth the Magi had presented the gift of myrrh (Matthew 2:11) commonly used when wrapping a body in the burial shroud, which foreshadowed Jesus' death. Now Jesus attached the same significance to Mary's deed of anointing him with pure nard.

Mary's gesture was spontaneous, probably done on the spur of the moment, yet it grew out of a long-practiced attentiveness to Jesus. The apostles had not understood when Jesus spoke directly to them about his impending passion (Luke 18:31-34). But perhaps Mary, with her fine sensitivity, sensed that he was troubled by the trials through which he was soon to pass and thus sought to comfort him with this loving favor.

Little did Mary imagine as she knelt at the feet of Jesus, anointing them and wiping them with her hair, that her action would become famous and her name known for generations to come. Her sole thought was to show the Lord how much she loved him. Treasuring her love, Jesus honored Mary and promised that "wherever this gospel is preached in the whole world, what she has done will be told in memory of her" (Matthew 26:13; Mark 14:9). In the spreading of the story of Mary's beautiful deed throughout the whole world—prefigured by the spreading of the sweet fragrance of the perfume throughout the house (John 12:3)—Jesus' prophecy has indeed been richly fulfilled:

Wherever in the world you may go, everyone respectfully listens to the story of her good service. . . . And yet hers was not an extraordinary deed, nor was she a distinguished person, nor was there a large audience, nor was the place one where she could easily be seen. She made no entrance onto a theater stage to perform her service but did her good deed in a private house. Nevertheless . . . today she is more illustrious than any king or queen; no passage of years has buried in oblivion this service she performed. (St. John Chrysostom, *Adversus Iudaeos*, V, 2)

Pondering the Word

1. What insight does the story in Luke 10:38-42 give you into Mary's personality? Martha's? In what ways were these sisters' responses to Jesus' visit similar? Different?

_____

_____

_____

_____

_____

_____

_____

_____

_____

2. What does Jesus' reply to Martha (Luke 10:41-42) reveal about himself? About his outlook toward others and his concern for them?

_____

_____

_____

_____

_____

_____

_____

_____

_____

_____

_____

3. How would you describe the "good portion" Mary chose (Luke 10:42)? What do you think Jesus meant when he said that this portion "shall not be taken away from her"?

_____

_____

_____

_____

_____

_____

_____

_____

_____

4. What, in your opinion, was Mary's main intention in anointing Jesus with the costly oil? What emotions might she have experienced as she performed her deed?

_____

_____

_____

_____

_____

_____

_____

_____

_____

5. Jesus said Mary had done a "beautiful" thing for him (Matthew 26:10). What other adjectives would you use to describe Mary's gesture?

_____

_____

_____

_____

_____

_____

_____

_____

_____

6. Read Mark 14:6-9 and list each element of Jesus' reply to the disciples' complaint that Mary had wasted the perfume. In what ways did Jesus' perspective on Mary's action and his interpretation of it differ from that of his disciples? Do you think Mary understood what Jesus said about her deed? Why or why not?

_____

_____

_____

_____

_____

_____

_____

_____

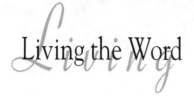

Living the Word

1. Imagine how you would go about welcoming Jesus into your home as a guest. What would be your main concern? Your main preoccupation? What would you do to prepare for his visit?

_____

_____

_____

_____

_____

_____

_____

_____

2. In what areas of your life are you like Martha, worried or preoccupied? Why? What can you do to find peace and freedom from your anxiety?

_____

_____

_____

_____

_____

_____

_____

_____

3. In what ways have you chosen the "good portion"? What role does reading and listening to God's word play in your life? How do you spend "quality time" with Jesus?

_____

_____

_____

_____

_____

_____

_____

_____

_____

_____

4. Often gestures speak more loudly than words. What, in particular, does Mary's anointing of Jesus say to you? What "beautiful" thing have you done to show Jesus your love for him?

_____

_____

_____

_____

_____

_____

_____

_____

_____

_____

_____

5. Are you generous in prayer? In service to others? In using your talents and skills for the Lord's work? In what areas are you self-protective or hesitant to "pour" yourself out? Why?

_____

_____

_____

_____

_____

_____

_____

_____

6. Certain things must be done immediately when the opportunity arises—like Mary anointing Jesus—or the moment will pass by. Have you ever acted on a spontaneous impulse to be generous? What happened?

_____

_____

_____

_____

_____

_____

_____

_____

Rooted in the Word

Mary of Bethany: A Portrait of Loving Attentiveness

Mary of Bethany's posture sitting at the feet of Jesus outwardly reflected her inner disposition: She gave him her fullest attention, put him first in her heart, and was eager to hear his word and learn from him. Her single-heartedness and "undivided devotion" (1 Corinthians 7:35) to Jesus made her especially sensitive to him. Surely we can assume from this disposition that Mary was attuned to him and his needs and ready to do whatever he might ask of her.

Mary's attentiveness to Jesus and her availability to him are also evident in the story of the raising of her brother Lazarus from the dead. John tells us that Mary had stayed behind grieving in the house, allowing Martha to speak with Jesus first as he arrived on the outskirts of the village (John 11:20, 30). But when Martha told her, "The Teacher is here and is calling for you," Mary responded immediately to her master's request, rising quickly to go to meet him (11:28-29). "Then Mary, when she came where Jesus was and saw him, fell at his feet" (11: 32).

This simple, straightforward exchange between Jesus and Mary can be a model for us in our own responsiveness to the Lord. We are to make ourselves available to Jesus, ready to answer his call and his wishes at all times. That includes those difficult times when we are weighed down by some concern or sorrow, as when Mary was mourning for Lazarus. But we also need to carve out time to sit at Jesus' feet in the course of our day-to-day lives, like Mary when Jesus visited her house for refreshment.

Read and prayerfully reflect on these additional Scripture passages that portray hearts lovingly attentive to God and responsive to him and to his word:

[David's last instructions to his son Solomon:] "Know the God of your father, and serve him with a whole heart and with a willing mind; for the LORD searches all hearts, and understands every plan and thought." (1 Chronicles 28:9)

One thing have I asked of the LORD,
    that will I seek after;
that I may dwell in the house of the LORD
    all the days of my life,
to behold the beauty of the LORD,
    and to inquire in his temple.
Thou hast said, "Seek ye my face."
    My heart says to thee,

"Thy face, LORD, do I seek."
    Hide not thy face from me.
(Psalm 27:4, 8-9)

Sacrifice and offering thou dost not
        desire;
    but thou hast given me an open ear.
Burnt offering and sin offering
    thou hast not required.
Then I said, "Lo, I come;
    in the roll of the book it is written
        of me;
I delight to do thy will, O my God;
    thy law is within my heart."
(Psalm 40:6-8)

I will meditate on thy precepts,
    and fix my eyes on thy ways.
I will delight in thy statutes;
    I will not forget thy word.
(Psalm 119:15-16)

[Jesus said:] "Blessed are the pure in heart, for they shall see God." (Matthew 5:8)

One of the scribes came up and heard them disputing with one another, and seeing that [Jesus] answered them well, asked him, "Which commandment is the first of all?" Jesus answered, "The first is, 'Hear, O Israel: The Lord our God, the Lord is one; and you shall love the Lord your God with all your heart, and with all your soul, and with all your mind, and with all your strength.' " (Mark 12:28-30)

Treasuring the Word

A Reading from *Three Women and the Lord* by Adrienne von Speyr

Mary of Bethany: Love

And she had a sister called Mary, who sat at the Lord's feet and listened to his teaching. It is the most natural thing in the world for Mary to sit at the Lord's feet. It is the first thing we hear of her, her introduction, her distinguishing mark. It is her character, her temperament. She sits at his feet, just as, in succeeding ages, all forms of contemplative life in the Church will sit at his feet: in order to look up to him—not to see him one-sidedly, but to be in the right place for listening to his word. He himself is the Word: he not only corresponds to it, he is identical with it. What Mary does is a response to this fact: she wants to make room for this fact with her whole being. She not only wants to hear the word; by listening she wants to receive the Lord into herself, she wants to be his vessel. Martha received him into her house externally. Mary receives him into the house of her own self. This space is free and available within her because her love makes it so and because she herself is drawn into it. And since it is there exclusively to receive the Lord, it is perfectly natural for her to sit down at his feet.

It is equally natural for the Lord to begin to speak. It is his response to the conditions he has created. He takes possession of the space he has prepared. And if, while he was journeying from place to place, love was like an invisible ray of light that, constantly in motion, struck no surface, now, suddenly, it shines out brilliantly, having encountered a listener who can receive it. If the love that pours from him is to become visible, it needs the answering love of the one who receives him. This love, which is continually nourished and is continually growing as a result of what he brings to it, is like a lamp that he has entrusted to Mary's care. She is the guardian of his love because she already loves. It is given to her because she already *has*. She is both like the rich man to whom riches are given and the poor man from whom is taken away "even that which he hath"— out of love for love, so that love may flourish. At first, love is as it were latent: the Lord, journeying here and there, is its pure, invisible radiance, and Mary is its pure, invisible expectation. Martha's action releases it into visibility, causing its hidden energy to explode.

. . . and listened to his teaching. Mary listens to the words pouring forth, she hears them in their fresh, dynamic originality.

Every one of the Lord's words is stamped with this same fundamental quality: as an expression of eternally valid truth and being, each word is primal, of the fountainhead and at the same time in dynamic process. The Lord stands at the center of his self-revelation; out of love he continually creates new expressions of love that men can understand, and his word will be a fountain in this way until the end of the world. This is because the Lord is what he says. In receiving his word, Mary receives the Lord's being. His word nourishes her contemplation of his being, and since it is of the essence of the Son to contemplate the Father in the Spirit and to strive toward him, he develops these same proportions in Mary's contemplation too. In her, the word is heard, the Word contemplated, is open to the infinity of the Divine Being in an openness that is one with love.

Judas

See, my betrayer is at hand.
Matthew 26:46

[Judas] was sorry for his act of madness, but he did not exercise the virtue of hope—for he could still have gained Our Lord's forgiveness—and he lacked the humility to return to Christ. He could have been one of the twelve founders of the Church despite the enormity of his guilt if he had asked God for forgiveness.
Francis Fernandez, *In Conversation with God*

The Judas in Me

Forgive my betrayals, Lord:

Those countless times
when I've slighted you
and turned away at your approach;
denied any knowledge of you by my nervous silence,
too embarrassed to stand up or speak for you;
or feigned false ignorance and bland disinterest,
failing to admit my allegiance to you and all my heart's devotion.

Forgive the Judas in me
(and the Peter, too)
when I fall short
and save me from despair
as I shed now these tears of shame and sorrow
for my disloyalties to you.

The Scene

Luke 22:1-6

22:1 Now the feast of Unleavened Bread drew near, which is called the Passover. 2 And the chief priests and the scribes were seeking how to put him to death; for they feared the people. 3 Then Satan entered into Judas called Iscariot, who was of the number of the twelve; 4 he went away and conferred with the chief priests and officers how he might betray him to them. 5 And they were glad, and engaged to give him money. 6 So he agreed, and sought an opportunity to betray him to them in the absence of the multitude.

The Scene

Matthew 26:20-25, 36, 45-50

26:20 When it was evening, [Jesus] sat at table with the twelve disciples; 21 and as they were eating, he said, "Truly, I say to you, one of you will betray me." 22 And they were very sorrowful, and began to say to him one after another, "Is it I, Lord?" 23 He answered, "He who has dipped his hand in the dish with me, will betray me. 24 The Son of man goes as it is written of him, but woe to that man by whom the Son of man is betrayed! It would have been better for that man if he had not been born." 25 Judas, who betrayed him, said, "Is it I, Master?" He said to him, "You have said so."

36 Then Jesus went with [his disciples] to a place called Gethsemane and he said to [them]: 45 ". . . Behold, the hour is at hand, and the Son of man is betrayed into the hands of sinners. 46 Rise, let us be going; see, my betrayer is at hand."

47 While he was still speaking, Judas came, one of the twelve, and with him a great crowd with swords and clubs, from the chief priests and the elders of the people. 48 Now the betrayer had given them a sign, saying, "The one I shall kiss is the man; seize him." 49 And he came up to Jesus at once and said, "Hail, Master!" And he kissed him. 50 Jesus said to him, "Friend, why are you here?" Then they came up and laid hands on Jesus and seized him.

13:21 [Jesus] was troubled in spirit, and testified, "Truly, truly, I say to you, one of you will betray me." 22 The disciples looked at one another, uncertain of whom he spoke. 23 One of his disciples, whom Jesus loved, was lying close to the breast of Jesus; 24 so Simon Peter beckoned to him and said, "Tell us who it is of whom he speaks." 25 So lying thus, close to the breast of Jesus, he said to him, "Lord, who is it?" 26 Jesus answered, "It is he to whom I shall give this morsel when I have dipped it." So when he had dipped the morsel, he gave it to Judas, the son of Simon Iscariot. 27 Then after the morsel, Satan entered into him. Jesus said to him, "What you are going to do, do quickly." 28 Now no one at the table knew why he said this to him. 29 Some thought that, because Judas had the money box, Jesus was telling him, "Buy what we need for the feast"; or, that he should give something to the poor. 30 So, after receiving the morsel, he immediately went out; and it was night.

18:1 [Jesus] went forth with his disciples across the Kidron valley, where there was a garden, which he and his disciples entered. 2 Now Judas, who betrayed him, also knew the place; for Jesus often met there with his disciples. 3 So Judas, procuring a band of soldiers and some officers from the chief priests and the Pharisees, went there with lanterns and torches and weapons. 4 Then Jesus, knowing all that was to befall him, came forward and said to them, "Whom do you seek?" 5 They answered him, "Jesus of Nazareth." Jesus said to them, "I am he." Judas, who betrayed him, was standing with them. 6 When he said to them, "I am he," they drew back and fell to the ground. 7 Again he asked them, "Whom do you seek?" And they said, "Jesus of Nazareth." 8 Jesus answered, "I told you that I am he."

See also Mark 14:10-11, 17-21, 43-50; Luke 22:21-23, 47-53

Reflecting on the Word

John the Evangelist gave us a privileged look at how the Lord spent the last evening of his life: "Jesus, knowing that the Father had given all things into his hands, and that he had come from God and was going to God, rose from supper, laid aside his garments, and girded himself with a towel" (John 13:3-4). Out of love for his friends, he washed their feet (13:5). Later, during dinner, "one of his disciples, whom Jesus loved, was lying close to the breast of Jesus" (13:23). This second glimpse into the depth of Jesus' friendship with his apostles most likely refers to the evangelist himself.

But a discordant note jarred this intimate circle of friends: "Troubled in spirit," Jesus told his chosen companions that one of them was going to betray him (John 13:21). "Very sorrowful"—and surely disturbed and bewildered—the disciples "began to say to him, one after another, 'Is it I, Lord?' " (Matthew 26:22). Why did they pose this question? As Archbishop Fulton Sheen commented:

> In the presence of Divinity, no one can be sure of his innocence, and everyone asked, "Is it I?" Every man is a mystery to himself, for he knows that within his heart there lie, coiled and dormant, serpents that at any moment would sting a neighbor with their poison, or even God. One of them could be sure that he was the traitor, and yet no one could be sure that he was not. (*Life of Christ*)

Indeed, we are all weak, and the deceit in our hearts is often unknown to us. Nonetheless God, who knows us better than we know ourselves, still loves us and has mercy on us.

Judas had successfully kept his devious plan—and perhaps the disdain for Jesus that had grown in him over the months—hidden from the other disciples. Now he feigned innocence and shock as he too asked, "Is it I, Master?" along with the others (Matthew 26:25). What a clever actor he must have been! And yet, Judas could not hide from Jesus, who already knew what was lurking in his heart.

The name of Judas has become a synonym for treachery. According to the dictionary, a "judas" is "a person who betrays under the guise of friendship." Jesus was deeply grieved that one whom he called a friend would conspire against him: "Even my bosom friend in whom I trusted, who ate of my bread, has lifted his heel against me" (Psalm 41:9; John 13:18). Perhaps as he washed Judas' feet, Jesus was hoping to win him over with this expression of love. In the ancient world, it was a sign of special favor when the host offered the choicest piece of food to a guest, so during the Passover meal, Jesus appealed to Judas in this way, too (John 13:26). Yet Judas determinedly refused each overture of reconciling love. "After the morsel, Satan entered into him" (13:27).

"Judas had closed his heart to Jesus, and

Satan moved in. Jesus recognized that surge of evil presence. He would not force the will of Judas, so he permitted him to pursue his treacherous goal," noted author Alfred McBride, O. Praem. Jesus instructed Judas, 'What you are going to do, do quickly' (John 13:27). As if to stress the darkness of evil, John wrote, "So, . . . he immediately went out; and it was night" (13:30).

To underscore Judas' breach of friendship, John explained that Judas knew exactly where to find Jesus—as one of his apostles, he had often been in Gethsemane with him (John 18:2). Even when the traitor arrived in the garden with a band of soldiers and betrayed his master brazenly with a kiss, "Jesus addresses him still—and, it would seem, always—as: Friend [Matthew 26:50]. Judas may have turned away from Jesus, but Jesus has not turned away from Judas" (Sister Wendy Beckett, *Sister Wendy's Nativity*).

The soldiers who came to arrest him were armed with weapons, yet Jesus is the one who remained in charge of the whole scene and confronted them first with the question, "Whom do you seek?" To their reply, "Jesus the Nazorean," he responded with the deeper truth of his identity, "I AM" (John 18:3-5). By using this form of God's revelation of his name to Moses (Exodus 3:13-14), Jesus clearly identified himself as God. Earlier he had told his adversaries, "When you have lifted up the Son of man, then you will know that I am he [I AM], and that I do nothing on my own authority. . . . He who has sent me is with me; he has not left me alone, for I always do what is pleasing to him" (John 8:28-29). Jesus went forward to his death in the sure knowledge that he was pleasing the Father.

We can only guess at the reasons for Judas' betrayal. Was it greed? In Matthew's and Mark's Gospels, his treachery begins to unfold after the anointing in Bethany (Matthew 26:6-16; Mark 14:3-11). In John's account of the anointing, he noted that it was Judas who complained that such expensive ointment should have been sold, and the proceeds given to the poor. Then John added, "This he said, not that he cared for the poor but because he was a thief, and as he had the money box he used to take what was put into it" (John 12:4-6). St. Leo the Great described Judas as "inflamed with the torch of greed" and so "ablaze to gain thirty pieces of silver" that he did not see the riches of Christ he was forfeiting (*Letters and Sermons*, Sermon 67). Ironically, it was for the price assigned to the life of a slave (see Exodus 21:32) that Judas sold Jesus.

Perhaps Judas turned against Jesus when he declared, ". . . Unless you eat the flesh of the Son of man and drink his blood, you have no life in you" (John 6:53). There were some among Jesus' disciples who took offense at him and this teaching at that time, and "Jesus knew from the first who those were that did not believe, and who it was that would betray him" (6:64).

Was Judas disappointed and disillusioned because Jesus had failed to reveal himself as a political Messiah? Or, in some twisted way, perhaps Judas thought that he could cleverly force Jesus into a situation where he would have to act in power to save himself, thus fulfilling his mission, as Judas understood it, to save Israel. The fact that Judas committed suicide after realizing that Jesus was condemned to death tends to support this possibility.

The gospels tell us too little to definitively judge Judas' motives. However, we do know that someone who had been so intimately associated with Jesus was still able to misunderstand him and fall prey to Satan (John 13:21). This should serve as a warning to us not to harden our hearts against Jesus' love, and to be aware of our own vulnerability to sin. As art historian Sr. Wendy Beckett cautions:

> The horror of Judas is not that he was unlike the other disciples but that he was just like them. He enjoyed all their advantages, above all the personal closeness to Jesus. Yet he could choose to deny him.
>
> We are being asked here to examine not the problem of Judas and his sin but the problem of our own: why do we betray, and walk away? (*Sister Wendy's Nativity*)

Matthew's is the sole Gospel to tell us that Judas, remorseful and despairing, ended his own life:

> When Judas, his betrayer, saw that he was condemned, he repented and brought back the thirty pieces of silver to the chief priests and the elders, saying, "I have sinned in betraying innocent blood." They said, "What is that to us? See to it yourself." And throwing down the pieces of silver in the temple, he departed; and he went and hanged himself. (Matthew 27:3-5)

Pondering the Word

1. What indications are there in the gospels of Judas' character? Of how he arrived at his plan to betray Jesus?

_____

_____

_____

_____

_____

_____

_____

_____

2. What choices, personal responsibility, and exercise of free will were involved in Judas' act of betrayal? What part did Satan play in it? Read Matthew 26:24, Luke 22:3, 22, John 13:27, and 1 Peter 5:8-9 as you consider your answers to these questions.

_____

_____

_____

_____

_____

_____

_____

_____

3. Earlier Jesus said, "No one takes [my life] from me, but I lay it down of my own accord. I have power to lay it down, and I have power to take it again; this charge I have received from my Father" (John 10:18). In light of Judas' actions, what does this suggest to you? What does it indicate about Jesus' role in God's plan to redeem humankind?

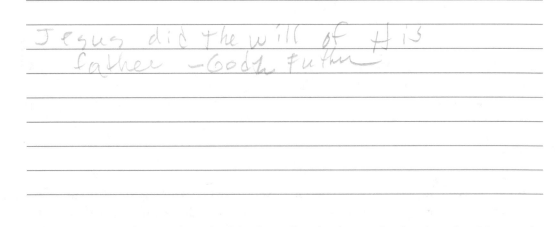

Jesus did the will of His father —God the Father

4. What reasons might Jesus have had for foretelling his betrayal to his disciples? How might the disciples have reacted if they had understood Judas' intentions when he left the supper (John 13:28-30)?

5. Jesus was "troubled in spirit" (John 13:21) before he was betrayed. What does this indicate to you about Jesus' human nature and about his feelings toward Judas? Toward his impending death? Toward his mission as Savior?

_____

_____

_____

_____

_____

_____

_____

6. Why do you think that Judas called Jesus "innocent" after he had betrayed him (Matthew 27:3-4)? Do you think he had anticipated the results of his treacherous act? In your opinion, why did Judas hang himself?

_____

_____

_____

_____

_____

_____

_____

Living the Word

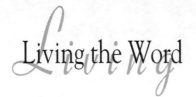

1. Judas may have been disturbed that Jesus didn't do what he expected of him. When have you felt disappointed that God didn't act according to your own plans or hopes? What did you do then?

_____

_____

_____

_____

_____

_____

_____

_____

_____

2. Have you ever experienced Satan tempting you to sin? If so, how were you made aware of Satan's role in the situation? How did you protect yourself?

_____

_____

_____

_____

_____

_____

_____

_____

_____

3. What evil forces do you recognize at work in the world today? Using Jesus as a model, how can Christians best confront evil?

_____

_____

_____

_____

_____

_____

_____

_____

_____

4. Have you ever been deeply hurt or betrayed by someone close to you? Have you needed God's help more than once to love and forgive that person?

_____

_____

_____

_____

_____

_____

_____

_____

_____

_____

5. Do you find it difficult to believe or accept that God forgives your sins? If so, why? When have you most deeply experienced God's forgiveness?

_____

_____

_____

_____

_____

_____

_____

_____

_____

6. Write a prayer expressing your sorrow and repentance for times you have "betrayed" God by failing to believe and trust in him or by failing to live according to his ways. Then praise and thank God for his mercy and forgiveness.

_____

_____

_____

_____

_____

_____

_____

_____

_____

Rooted in the Word

Judas: A Portrait of Regret

How terribly Judas' sin must have weighed on him! Recognizing the magnitude of the evil he had done, he regretted that he had betrayed Jesus. Judas' regret, however, did not lead to a change of heart and to a repentance that sought forgiveness. It was, rather, a regret of the consequences of his sin—and a disgust and self-hatred that led him to despair and to self-destruction.

Instead of focusing on God, asking pardon, and trusting in his love, Judas focused on himself and on the weight of the sin crushing him. Guilt must have been devouring him so voraciously that he forgot all that Jesus had taught him and the other disciples about the mercy of God. His betrayal loomed so large before his eyes that he was blinded to Jesus' love. Despair tightened its hold on him so strongly that any hope of forgiveness was strangled. Tragically, Judas took his own life.

In his commentary on Judas' end as recorded in Matthew's Gospel (27:3-10), Alfred McBride points to the sickness of despair:

> While [Judas] had the decency to acknowledge the innocence of Jesus, he lacked the sublimity of faith that would have rescued him from the despair that drove him to suicide. He never appreciated the offer of forgiveness that was central to the mission of Jesus. Christ would be nailed to the tree of hope. Judas died on the tree of despair. (*The Kingdom and the Glory*)

Peter, too, had denied the Lord, but he did not allow his regret to turn him away from the Lord. "Jesus' look of infinite mercy [Luke 22:61-62] drew tears of repentance from Peter" (*Catechism of the Catholic Church*, 1429). He acknowledged his failing and trusted in God's forgiveness and mercy. Peter's sorrow was the "godly grief [that] produces a repentance that leads to salvation and brings no regret, but worldly grief produces death" (2 Corinthians 7:10). Judas knew only an ungodly grief and despaired.

Read and prayerfully reflect on these additional Scripture passages that describe the pardon and joy that follow from true repentance and the confession of sin:

> Blessed is he whose transgression is
>   forgiven,
>   whose sin is covered.
> Blessed is the man to whom the LORD

imputes no iniquity,
  and in whose spirit there is no
    deceit.
When I declared not my sin, my body
    wasted away
  through my groaning all day long.
For day and night thy hand was heavy
    upon me;
  my strength was dried up as by the
    heat of summer.
I acknowledged my sin to thee,
  and I did not hide my iniquity;
I said, "I will confess my transgres
    sions to the LORD";
  then thou didst forgive the guilt of
    my sin.
Therefore let every one who is godly
  offer prayer to thee;
at a time of distress, in the rush of
    great waters,
  they shall not reach him.
Thou art a hiding place for me,
  thou preservest me from trouble;
  thou dost encompass me with
    deliverance.
  (Psalm 32:1-7)

He who conceals his transgressions
    will not prosper,
  but he who confesses and forsakes
    them will obtain mercy.
  (Proverbs 28:13)

Thus says the LORD,
  your Redeemer, the Holy One of
    Israel:
"I, I am He
  who blots out your transgressions
    for my own sake,
  and I will not remember your sins."
(Isaiah 43:14, 25)

[Jesus said:] "I tell you, there will be more joy in heaven over one sinner who repents than over ninety-nine righteous persons who need no repentance." (Luke 15:7)

[Peter addressed the people, saying:] "And now, brethren, I know that you acted in ignorance, as did also your rulers. But what God foretold by the mouth of all the prophets, that his Christ should suffer, he thus fulfilled. Repent therefore, and turn again, that your sins may be blotted out, that times of refreshing may come from the presence of the Lord." (Acts 3:17-19)

If we confess our sins, he is faithful and just, and will forgive our sins and cleanse us from all unrighteousness. (1 John 1:9)

Treasuring the Word

A Reading from *Who Do You Say I Am?* by Ralph Martin

Judas—So Near and Yet So Far

Most of us do not identify with Judas. We find it difficult to imagine why this disciple would betray the Messiah. Jesus did not choose Judas because he would make a good villain. He chose him because he loved him. And Judas chose to walk with Jesus because he wanted to know the truth. Judas was served by the Master even unto the end when he washed Judas' feet at the Last Supper. Judas saw Jesus' miracles, he knew his character, sincerity, and wisdom. Not only did Judas see all the works of Jesus, he also participated in them, feeding the five thousand and healing the sick. The power of God flowed through him as he used the name of Jesus. He even reported to Jesus how demons were subjected to him. People were healed when he prayed. So what happened to Judas? How did he come to betray his Lord? . . .

The devil was looking for weaknesses in Jesus' disciples, for their natural tendencies toward pride, greed, doubt, jealousy, envy, and fear. Probing their defenses for a way to get at them, Satan discovered in Judas an opening through which he could influence and enslave him, and finally drive him to betrayal.

Although all the disciples had weaknesses, the devil found a particularly vulnerable area in Judas' life. Little by little, over a period of time, Judas began to entertain evil thoughts, to give in to selfish emotions, to harden his heart towards Jesus. We can only speculate as to what exactly went on inside Judas, but what we can surmise sheds light on our own vulnerabilities. . . .

Being a disciple of Jesus had become more difficult, and perhaps Judas was just growing weary of doing good. Galatians 6:9 tells us, "Let us not grow weary of well-doing. . . ." Why? Because we, like Judas, have a tremendous tendency to grow weary in doing good, especially when it begins to cost us. Whether we have followed Jesus for one year or sixty years, we can tire of living righteously. Must we always do what is right, even if it involves suffering? Perhaps Judas finally decided that he had simply had enough of goodness, faith, and obedience. Wasn't it time to take matters into his own hands and avoid the trouble that loomed ahead? . . .

From Matthew 26:1-16 we know that the final straw that provoked Judas to action occurred when a woman came in and, to everyone's indignation, poured a costly ointment on Jesus' head. As the treasurer of Jesus' band, Judas knew all too well what this ointment was worth. It is likely that he was infuriated by this extravagant waste. If he could have sold the ointment, think of all the ways the disciples could have used it.

Are Judas' motives so far removed from our own? We too are tempted to look at life from the world's perspective and watch enviously as others rise to power, acquire worldly possessions, and get ahead in business. The choice between seeking first the kingdom of God and getting ahead in this world can arouse incredible conflict within us. Like Judas, are we not tempted at times to see our choice for Christ as an extravagant waste? Many of us are.

So Judas betrayed Jesus for money, for thirty pieces of silver—and with a kiss (Matthew 26:48-50). In this embrace, Judas betrayed the one who loved him and called him into an intimate relationship. He perverted this sacred sign of friendship and love. Think of the heartache Jesus must have experienced when he received this empty gesture, knowing well that Judas had rejected the love of God for the love of a few pieces of silver. Considering the fact that the precious ointment with which the woman anointed Jesus earlier was worth three hundred pieces of silver, Judas sold Jesus at a cheap price. He betrayed Jesus for almost nothing! . . .

After Jesus was arrested and the chief priests took formal action against him to put him to death, it looked as though Judas may have had a change of heart: "Judas, who had handed him over, seeing that Jesus had been condemned, began to regret his action deeply. He took the thirty pieces of silver back to the chief priests and elders and said, 'I did wrong to deliver up an innocent man!' " (Matthew 27:4). . . . At this moment of regret, it seems that Satan loosened his deceptive hold on Judas, and he came to his senses.

But the damage was done. The chief priests were not interested in whether Jesus was an innocent man. They were interested only in killing him. . . .

Judas realized the evil of his choices. But instead of repenting and turning to Jesus to ask forgiveness, his self-sufficient pride told him, "My sin is too great; I can't be forgiven." Giving in to despair, he hanged himself.

Doubt, pride, and deception knock at the door of our hearts as well. Even those of us who have followed Jesus for a long time and seen his power working through us must take heed lest we fall. Just as the devil waited for an opportune time to deceive Judas, so he waits to take advantage of us. That moment when we weary of doing good, when we doubt the words of Jesus, when we wonder when his promises will be fulfilled, when we fear the scandal of the cross, in that moment we can become the betrayer ourselves.

Joseph of Arimathea and Nicodemus

Joseph of Arimathea . . . took courage and went to Pilate, and asked for the body of Jesus.
Mark 15:43

There is a kind of splendor in Joseph of Arimathea finding the courage to profess his faith in Christ at the moment when Christ had seemed to have gone down in total failure. What is equally remarkable is that that other cautious member of the Sanhedrin, Nicodemus, found *his* courage in the same bleak moment.
F. J. Sheed, *To Know Christ Jesus*

Laid to Rest

The women keep silent vigil,
watching over the sagging, twisted body
hanging limply now upon the cross.
Light and life and breath are gone from his frame.
Stillness reigns, bringing with it
relief from the heavy horror of the day's events.

Joseph of Arimathea bravely declares himself,
claiming in death what he had feared in life.
He unfastens the broken body from the crossbeam,
careful not to further wound
the flesh so bruised and torn by nails.
What reverence for the tabernacle
that gave human form to God!

Mary cradles her son in her arms as she so often had
when he laid his soft infant cheek upon her breast.
Her hand gently caresses the bloodied, cold brow
and tenderly closes the sightless eyes
before she gives him over to the grave.

(Mary, what were your thoughts then?
Did your son's words of life and resurrection
echo in your ears?
Beneath your grief and sorrow,
did hope that he might rise and live again
stir deeply in your mother's heart
and sustain you in quiet expectation?)

Now he rests from salvation's work and pain,
the sleep of death upon him as he's enshrouded in linen.

Sweet spices surround and perfume his wounded corpse.

Darkness falls as the stone is rolled in place.
Yet a deeper darkness invades and fills the rock-hewn sepulchre,
reaching into its narrow confines
and encircling the body it now holds as in a womb.

Soon morning light will dawn upon the stone-cold tomb,
warming its icy hardness.
But greater light shines from within,
glowing and pulsing with new life and waiting to find release.
No guard set there to vigilantly keep watch
(and hold death within its chamber)
will stay his power to burst forth.

For he has torn, that he may heal us;
he has stricken, and he will bind us up.
After two days he will revive us;
on the third day he will raise us up,
that we may live before him. . . .
His going forth is as sure as the dawn.

O Sun of Righteousness,
night's shadows must fade before the glory of your rising.
Triumph now over death's dark domain,
and spread the radiance of your newly won dominion over us!

Luke 23:50-56 *The Scene*

23:50 Now there was a man named Joseph from the Jewish town of Arimathea. He was a member of the council, a good and righteous man, 51 who had not consented to their purpose and deed, and he was looking for the kingdom of God. 52 This man went to Pilate and asked for the body of Jesus. 53 Then he took it down and wrapped it in a linen shroud, and laid him in a rock-hewn tomb, where no one had ever yet been laid. 54 It was the day of Preparation, and the sabbath was beginning. 55 The women who had come with him from Galilee followed, and saw the tomb, and how his body was laid; 56 then they returned, and prepared spices and ointments. On the sabbath they rested according to the commandment.

135

John 19:38-42 *The Scene*

19:38 Joseph of Arimathea, who was a disciple of Jesus, but secretly, for fear of the Jews, asked Pilate that he might take away the body of Jesus, and Pilate gave him leave. So he came and took away his body. 39 Nicodemus also, who had at first come to him by night, came bringing a mixture of myrrh and aloes, about a hundred pounds' weight. 40 They took the body of Jesus, and bound it in linen cloths with the spices, as is the burial custom of the Jews. 41 Now in the place where he was crucified there was a garden, and in the garden a new tomb where no one had ever been laid. 42 So because of the Jewish day of Preparation, as the tomb was close at hand, they laid Jesus there.

See also Matthew 27:57-61;
Mark 15:42-47

Reflecting on the Word

Joseph of Arimathea had been a secret disciple of Jesus, too fearful to openly declare allegiance to the rabbi from Galilee and follow him. Nonetheless, he found the courage to disagree with the Sanhedrin's plan to have Jesus put to death (Luke 23:51). After the crucifixion, he boldly went to Pilate to claim Jesus' body for proper burial. Perhaps Joseph's thought was to give Jesus the honor at least in death that he had been afraid to show while he was alive. There was nothing else that he could now do.

Joseph was from the Jewish town of Arimathea (Luke 23:50), called Amartha by the Jewish historian Josephus. Some scholars identify this town with Ramatha, the birthplace of the prophet Samuel, while others associate it with present-day Ramallah, which is eight miles north of Jerusalem. Luke noted that Joseph was a "righteous" man (Luke 23:50), the same word he used to describe the parents of John the Baptist, Zechariah and Elizabeth (1:6), and Simeon (2:25). Joseph was waiting—just as Simeon and Anna (2:38) had been—for the reign of God. Matthew's Gospel refers to him as a wealthy man (Matthew 27:57), and both Mark and Luke identify him as a member of the Jewish council, the Sanhedrin (Mark 15:43; Luke 23:50).

Nicodemus, another prominent Jewish leader, assisted Joseph in this sorrowful hour after Jesus' closest disciples had fled. A Pharisee and teacher of Israel (John 3:1, 10), he had recognized Jesus as "a teacher come from God; for no one can do these signs that you do, unless God is with him" (3:2). Like Joseph, Nicodemus had been reluctant to publicly associate himself with Jesus and had come secretly at night to talk with him about the things of the Spirit (19:39). It is remarkable that both Nicodemus and Joseph came forth bravely to show their devotion to Jesus after he had been put to death by government authorities. The power of the cross was already at work to free their hearts from the bondage of fear.

The Mosaic law decreed that the body of a man put to death for his crimes "shall not remain all night upon the tree" but should be buried the same day (Deuteronomy 21:22-23). It was Jewish custom that the corpses of executed criminals be buried in common graves as a mark of disgrace. They would remain there until the flesh rotted away; only then could the bones of the executed be returned to their families. But Joseph asked Pilate's permission to give Jesus a decent burial. Refusing such a request or demanding money for returning a criminal's body to the family was considered by the Romans to be an exceptional severity, so Pilate—perhaps with a guilty conscience for putting an innocent man to death—gave Joseph his approval.

In his work *The Passion of the Lord*, sixteenth-century Jesuit Luis de la Palma wrote that Joseph made one of the greatest demands ever. He asked for "the Body of Jesus,

Son of God, treasure of the Church . . . the Bread which will sustain one until life eternal. In that moment Joseph, with his petition, represents the desires of all men, of the whole Church, which needs Him to keep eternally alive."

Having secured Pilate's permission, Joseph set about the harrowing work of unfastening the nails from the lifeless body that hung limply on the cross.

Once removed from the wooden beams, Jesus' body was washed and prepared for burial. Even though the law compassionately allowed for the embalming of the dead on the sabbath, Joseph worked hastily and chose to place the body in his own tomb, which was close by (John 19:42), because daylight was quickly fading.

Jesus' body was bound in a linen winding sheet, called the *sindon*, and his face was covered with a smaller piece of linen, the *soudarion* (see John 20:6-7). As Mary watched her son's body being wrapped in the shroud, perhaps she thought of how she had wrapped him as an infant in swaddling bands. Nicodemus added to Joseph's kind services, bringing spices to bind with the body in the shroud, as was the Jewish custom (John 19:39). At Jesus' birth the wise men had brought him costly gifts fit for a king—gold, frankincense, and myrrh (Matthew 2:11). Now John alludes at Jesus' death to his royal status by telling us that he was laid to rest with a hundred pounds' weight of myrrh and aloes.

Myrrh, the fragrant resinous gum of commiphora trees, was customarily crushed into a powder and mixed with aloes to sweeten the air about the tomb. It was not uncommon to use twenty to fifty pounds of the spices for funerals, and even much larger quantities were used for the renowned. For example, Herod the Great was buried beneath spices brought by five hundred slaves.

With the help of Nicodemus, Joseph laid Jesus' body in his own grave in a garden about thirty yards from Golgotha. The tomb was hewn out of the soft limestone so common around Jerusalem (Matthew 27:60). Ordinarily, tombs of the rich had an antechamber and an inner burial chamber with ledges or shelves around its walls. The bodies, wrapped in shrouds and spices, were laid on the shelves and more spices were poured around them. Finally, a large stone, fitting into a sleeve of rock, was rolled across the entrance to the tomb to seal it.

As St. Augustine wrote, "Just as in the womb of the Virgin Mary none was conceived before him, none after him, so in this tomb none before him, none after was buried" (*Tractate on the Gospel of John*, 120, 5). And with Jesus' burial in Joseph's tomb, another of the prophecies regarding the Messiah was fulfilled: "They made his grave . . . with a rich man in his death" (Isaiah 53:9).

Jesus' resurrection surely would have surprised Joseph and Nicodemus, since they had wrapped his dead body in the shroud themselves (John 19:40) and Joseph had rolled the stone in place across the entrance to the tomb (Mark 15:46). In fact, the evangelists gave so many details about Jesus' burial in order to establish the fact that he was indeed dead and to leave their readers with no doubt that his resurrection was genuine—"He has risen, as he said" (Matthew 28:6).

The witness of Joseph of Arimathea and Nicodemus reminds us that it is never too late to turn to the Lord with love and reverence. Tardy though they were in openly declaring themselves for Jesus, they were courageous and wholehearted in their subsequent devotion and were privileged to minister to the broken body of Christ, the "temple" that Jesus promised would be raised up in three days (Mark 14:58). Most likely, Joseph and Nicodemus became active members of the early church in Jerusalem.

The Church of the Holy Sepulchre in Jerusalem is built over the sites of Jesus' execution at Golgotha and his burial in a nearby garden. In the entranceway of the church, a flat marble slab has been placed to commemorate how Joseph and Nicodemus anointed Jesus' broken body for burial. Countless pilgrims pour out bottles of perfume or scatter flower petals to express their love and devotion to the Lord, just as Joseph and Nicodemus did as they buried their Savior. The names of Joseph of Arimathea and Nicodemus, and their generosity to the Lord, will always be remembered by all who know that death was not able to hold Jesus in the tomb where they once laid him.

Pondering the Word

1. What was the reaction of Joseph to Jesus' arrest and crucifixion? Of the women who were his followers? How do they differ from the apostles' reactions?

_____

_____

_____

_____

_____

_____

_____

_____

_____

2. List all the adjectives the evangelists used to describe Joseph of Arimathea. What impression do you have of him from these descriptive words?

_____

_____

_____

_____

_____

_____

_____

_____

_____

_____

_____

3. Read John 3:1-15, which relates Nicodemus' encounter with Jesus at night. What do you think Nicodemus was seeking? What does this encounter tell you about him?

_____

_____

_____

_____

_____

_____

_____

_____

_____

4. In your opinion, what was it about Jesus' death that made such an impact on Nicodemus and Joseph that they then acted openly?

_____

_____

_____

_____

_____

_____

_____

_____

5. What risks did Joseph and Nicodemus take by burying Jesus' body? What might have been some of the consequences—both positive and negative—of their action?

_____

_____

_____

_____

_____

_____

_____

6. Make note of all the "evidence" for Jesus' death that you find in the evangelists' descriptions of his burial. Where and how do you think they got the detailed information that they included in their gospels?

_____

_____

_____

_____

_____

_____

_____

_____

Living the Word

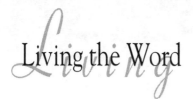

1. Have you ever hesitated to publicly identify yourself with Jesus? If so, why? Recall a situation in your life when you put yourself on the line for the Lord. What happened?

_____

_____

_____

_____

_____

_____

_____

_____

2. Joseph of Arimathea put himself at the service of Jesus at the darkest hour, without expecting any recompense. Have you ever helped someone in need, even when you felt discouraged by the challenges of his or her situation? What did you learn?

_____

_____

_____

_____

_____

_____

_____

_____

3. Are you facing any situation in your life in which Jesus seems to be "in the tomb," absent from you? How might Joseph's example help you when you feel this way?

_____

_____

_____

_____

_____

_____

_____

_____

4. Jesus' wounded, broken body reminds us of the divisions among Christians today. What can you do to foster unity among the various denominations in the Christian church, the broken body of Christ?

_____

_____

_____

_____

_____

_____

_____

_____

_____

5. Have you ever experienced the death of someone very close to you? What support did you value most from those around you? Did you learn anything then that can help you support others when they are grieving the loss of a loved one?

_____

_____

_____

_____

_____

_____

_____

_____

_____

6. Take some time to pray, perhaps kneeling before a crucifix, and imagine yourself removing Jesus' body from the cross and anointing him for burial. Write a short prayer expressing your love and devotion to Jesus.

_____

_____

_____

_____

_____

_____

_____

_____

_____

Joseph of Arimathea and Nicodemus:
Portraits of Generosity

Joseph made a gift of himself to God—risking his reputation, perhaps even his life—when he went to Pilate to claim Jesus' body for burial. Then he made a gift of his own tomb to Jesus. Nicodemus provided a hundredweight of spices for the burial, a quantity that would have cost an enormous sum. The most precious gifts are those given out of love, in a spirit of sacrifice and generosity.

When we are loving, we do not calculate or withhold. We are not tight-fisted or grudging. We do not seek our own advantage or look for gain or reward. Rather, when we love, we give liberally, open-handedly, even with reckless extravagance. We do not ask, "How little?" Rather, we ask, "How much?"

Truly generous people often deprive themselves or do with less in order to give more abundantly, like the poor widow who put two copper coins—her "whole living"—in the Temple treasury (Mark 12:41-44). What we have to offer may seem small or insignificant, but if we put all we have at the Lord's disposal, he can multiply its value and usefulness far more than we could imagine.

Generosity flows from a heart that is freely and wholly given to God—love responding to love. St. Ignatius of Loyola described that spirit in what has come to be known as his "Prayer for Generosity":

O my God, teach me to be generous:
to serve you as you deserve to be served;
to give without counting the cost;
to fight without fear of being wounded;
to work without seeking rest;
and to spend myself without expecting any
    reward,
but the knowledge that I am doing your
    holy will.

Read and prayerfully reflect on these additional Scripture passages about being generous toward the Lord and those in need:

[Moses summoned all Israel, and said to them:] "If there is among you a poor man, one of your brethren, in any of your towns within your land which the LORD your God gives you, you shall not harden your heart or shut your hand against your poor brother, but you shall open your hand to him, and lend him sufficient for his need, whatever it may be. . . . You shall give to him freely, and your heart shall not be grudging when you give to him; because for this the

LORD your God will bless you in all your work and in all that you undertake." (Deuteronomy 15:7-8, 10)

David blessed the LORD in the presence of all the assembly; and David said: ". . . Who am I, and what is my people, that we should be able thus to offer willingly? For all things come from thee, and of thy own have we given thee. For we are strangers before thee, and sojourners, as all our fathers were; our days on the earth are like a shadow, and there is no abiding. O LORD our God, all this abundance that we have provided for building thee a house for thy holy name comes from thy hand and is all thy own. I know, my God, that thou triest the heart, and hast pleasure in uprightness; in the uprightness of my heart I have freely offered all these things, and now I have seen thy people, who are present here, offering freely and joyously to thee." (1 Chronicles 29:10, 14-17)

A liberal man will be enriched,
    and one who waters will himself
        be watered.
(Proverbs 11:25)

[Jesus] sat down opposite the treasury, and watched the multitude putting money into the treasury. Many rich people put in large sums. And a poor widow came, and put in two copper coins, which make a penny. And he called his disciples to him, and said to them, "Truly, I say to you, this poor widow has put in more than all those who are contributing to the treasury. For they all contributed out of their abundance; but she out of her poverty has put in everything she had, her whole living." (Mark 12:41-44)

He who sows sparingly will also reap sparingly, and he who sows bountifully will also reap bountifully. Each one must do as he has made up his mind, not reluctantly or under compulsion, for God loves a cheerful giver. And God is able to provide you with every blessing in abundance, so that you may always have enough of everything and may provide in abundance for every good work. As it is written,
    "He scatters abroad, he gives to
        the poor;
        his righteousness endures for
ever."
He who supplies seed to the sower and bread for food will supply and multiply your resources and increase the harvest of your righteousness. (2 Corinthians 9:6-10)

As for the rich in this world, charge them not to be haughty, nor to set their hopes on uncertain riches but on God who richly furnishes us with everything to enjoy. They are to do good, to be rich in good deeds, liberal and generous, thus laying up for themselves a good foundation for the future, so that they may take hold of the life which is life indeed. (1 Timothy 6:17-19)

Treasuring the Word

A Reading from *Life of Christ* by Archbishop Fulton J. Sheen

The Night Friends of Christ

The body of the Savior hung limp upon the Cross—anybody's property, but it belonged to the mother especially. No one in all the world, except Mary, could pronounce His words at the Last Supper as she could, though she was not a priestess. Since no one but the Blessed Mother had given Him body and blood, the Holy Spirit overshadowing, only she could say: "This is my body; this is my blood." She alone gave Him that by which He redeemed; she alone made Him possible; she alone made Him the new Adam. There was no human counterpart; only the Spirit of Love.

Mary claimed Him as her own through the services of two rich men. One was Nicodemus, the secret disciple who made his appearances at night. Nicodemus was a doctor of the law and was looked upon as a master in Israel. From the very beginning, he knew that Our Savior was a teacher come from heaven, yet in order to preserve his authority and not expose himself to the hatred of his countrymen, he always showed up in darkness. The other, Joseph of Arimathea, gave Him the new tomb. The latter had gone to Pilate to ask him for the body of Our Lord, and Pilate committed it to him. The wealth, rank, and position of these men was noteworthy; one heard the Crucified One tell about His being "lifted up"; the other came from the land of mourning, the site of Rachel's tomb. Isaiah centuries before had foretold that Our Lord would be "rich in death"; He is now given over to the rich man, Joseph of Arimathea.

These two men with a few devout followers prepared to take Our Lord down, to unfasten the nails and take off the crown of thorns. Bending over the figure on which the Blood was hardened, only the eyes of faith could see the marks of royalty there. But with the love that broke through all bounds of calculation, these two latecomers and hidden disciples tried to show their loyalty. It is likely that when the dead Christ was taken down from the Cross, He was laid in the arms of His Blessed Mother. To a mother no child ever grows up. It must have seemed for the moment that Bethlehem had come back again, for He was a Babe in her embrace. But all had changed. He was no longer white as He came from the Father; He was red as He came from the hands of men.

Nicodemus and Joseph anointed the Body with a hundred pounds of myrrh and spices and wound it about with pure linen. The elaborate embalming rather suggested that these secret disciples, as the Apostles themselves, were not expecting the Resurrection. Physically, they were mindful of Him; spiritually, they knew not yet Who He was. Their concern about His burial was a token of their love for Him, not of their faith in Him as the Resurrection and Life.

. . . Born in a stranger's cave, buried in a stranger's grave, both human birth and death were strangers to His Divinity. Stranger's grave, too, because since sin was foreign to Him, so too was death. Dying for others, He was placed in another's grave. His grave was borrowed, for He would give it back on Easter.

Mary Magdalene

Woman, why are you weeping? Whom do you seek?
John 20:15

Jesus said to her: Mary! The word had that unique inflection which Jesus gives to every name—ours too!—and which goes hand in hand with a vocation, with a special friendship. Jesus calls us by our name and the tone of his voice is unmistakable.
Francis Fernandez, *In Conversation with God*

Awakened to Eternity

The day of rest past—
rest prescribed by law,
rest that refreshed her body
and eased the fatigue of the harrowing day spent at Golgotha,
yet brought no relief to her grief—
Mary made her way early
to the garden where the priceless treasure of her master's body lay,
that tabernacle so cruelly ransacked and emptied of the glow of life.

Night's veil was not yet lifted from the earth,
but already a faint glimmer spilled over the horizon's edge,
pushing back the shadows
and spreading its soft light through the garden as Mary entered there.
Yet even as the dawn began to break,
desolate darkness and black fear blinded her eyes,
for she'd come in one last act of kindness
to anoint her Beloved with sweet spices—
and found the tomb and grave cloths empty
and his body gone!

"O Gardener, tell me where you've laid my Lord,
that I might see him once again!"

Then Mary heard her name
as only *he* could speak it
and knew him in the sound of it.
Joy rushed in upon her,
and in the morning sun,
her heart was filled
(like the garden 'round about her)
with new life and vitality.

II

I too seek my Lord with love's longing.

Now go to him, my soul.
You'll find him (as Mary did so long ago)
waiting for you in the garden as in a lovers' trysting place.

In that fair place
where seed has fallen to its death
(buried in its own earthen grave beside his tomb)
and now springs forth in fruitfulness and fragrance,
he wipes away all tears
and speaks my name in a voice my ears have ever strained to hear,
restorer of my life
and herald of my wakening into eternity.

Luke 8:1-3 *The Scene*

8:1 Soon afterward [Jesus] went on through cities and villages, preaching and bringing the good news of the kingdom of God. And the twelve were with him, 2 and also some women who had been healed of evil spirits and infirmities: Mary, called Magdalene, from whom seven demons had gone out, 3 and Joanna, the wife of Chuza, Herod's steward, and Susanna, and many others, who provided for them out of their means.

John 20:1-18 *The Scene*

20:1 Now on the first day of the week Mary Magdalene came to the tomb early, while it was still dark, and saw that the stone had been taken away from the tomb. 2 So she ran, and went to Simon Peter and the other disciple, the one whom Jesus loved, and said to them, "They have taken the Lord out of the tomb, and we do not know where they have laid him." 3 Peter then came out with the other disciple, and they went toward the tomb. 4 They both ran, but the other disciple outran Peter and reached the tomb first; 5 and stooping to look in, he saw the linen cloths lying there, but he did not go in. 6 Then Simon Peter came, following him, and went into the tomb; he saw the linen cloths lying, 7 and the napkin, which had been on his head, not lying with the linen cloths but rolled up in a place by itself. 8 Then the other disciple, who reached the tomb first, also went in, and he saw and believed; 9 for as yet they did not know the scripture, that he must rise from the dead. 10 Then the disciples went back to their homes.

11 But Mary stood weeping outside the tomb, and as she wept she stooped to look into the tomb; 12 and she saw two angels in white, sitting where the body of Jesus had lain, one at the head and one at the feet. 13 They said to her, "Woman, why are you weeping?" She said to them, "Because they have taken away my Lord, and I do not know where they have laid him." 14 Saying this, she turned round and saw Jesus standing, but she did not know that it was Jesus. 15 Jesus said to her, "Woman, why are you weeping? Whom do you seek?" Supposing him to be the gardener, she said to him, "Sir, if you have carried him away, tell me where you have laid

him, and I will take him away." [16] Jesus said to her, "Mary." She turned and said to him in Hebrew, "Rabboni!" (which means Teacher). [17] Jesus said to her, "Do not hold me, for I have not yet ascended to the Father; but go to my brethren and say to them, I am ascending to my Father and your Father, to my God and your God." [18] Mary Magdalene went and said to the disciples, "I have seen the Lord"; and she told them that he had said these things to her.

Reflecting on the Word

Renaissance and Elizabethan Englanders called Mary Magdalene the "Mawdleyn," a version of her name that gave rise to the modern word "maudlin," which describes someone who weeps sentimentally. "Reformed prostitute" is the definition of "Magdalene" given by the *Concise Oxford Dictionary*. But do these images describe the true Magdalene of the gospels? Or has history falsely labeled—and thus badly maligned—this devoted follower of Jesus?

Most likely, the surname Magdalene indicates Mary's hometown. In first-century Palestine, Magdala was one of the largest towns around the Sea of Galilee. Archaeologists today identify it with the excavated ruins of Magdal, located not far from Tiberias, where the hills reach down to the lakeshore.

Plagued by evil spirits, Mary Magdalene was healed by Jesus (Luke 8:2). Consequently, some have concluded that she was emotionally unstable, a volatile personality—and wouldn't it then follow?—of questionable virtue. Adding to this impression, several early biblical commentators identified her with the unnamed penitent who anointed the feet of Jesus (7:36-50). While there's no evidence at all in the gospels that Mary and the repentant woman were the same person, Mary Magdalene nonetheless became the stereotype of a reformed sinner. Actually, there's no reason to think she had led an immoral life or been a prostitute. Rather, it's much more probable that she suffered from epileptic seizures or a mental disorder. In other scenes described by Luke, Jesus' casting out of evil spirits resulted in people being healed of epilepsy (9:38-42), the inability to speak (11:14), and curvature of the spine (13:10-13).

Mary Magdalene was among the women who accompanied Jesus in his public ministry. Perhaps some of these women were relatives of Jesus. They may have been wealthy, supporting Jesus and his disciples with their resources. Some were young, and others were middle-aged and had sons who also followed this itinerant rabbi. But all these women had one thing in common: Their hearts had been deeply touched by Jesus, and as a result, their lives were changed.

Mary was probably among the crowd of followers who praised Jesus as he triumphantly entered Jerusalem. Did she, like many others in the holy city, expect him to deliver Israel from the Roman occupation? Less than a week later, Jesus was seized in Gethsemane, and his closest male disciples "deserted him and ran away" (Matthew 26:56). Perhaps they ran to find Mary Magdalene and the other women who followed Jesus to tell them of the master's arrest.

We know from the gospels that there were women present at Golgotha: "There were many women there, looking on from a distance, who had followed Jesus from Galilee, ministering to him. Among them were Mary Magdalene and Mary the mother of James and Joseph, and the mother of the sons of Zebedee" (Matthew 27:55-56; see also Mark 15:40-41;

Luke 23:49). It is noteworthy that while many of the sons had fled, the mothers remained. John adds, "Standing by the cross of Jesus were his mother, and his mother's sister, Mary the wife of Clopas, and Mary Magdalene" (John 19:25).

Mary Magdalene and her companions watched as Joseph of Arimathea and Nicodemus removed Jesus' body from the cross and laid him in the tomb (Luke 23:50-56; see also Matthew 27:59-61 and Mark 15:46-47). After the sabbath, they returned to the tomb to anoint Jesus' body with spices (Matthew 28:1; Mark 16:1; Luke 24:1, 10). No thoughts of resurrection were in their minds. They hadn't understood Jesus' prophecies that he would be "raised on the third day" (Matthew 17:23; see also Mark 9:31). In their grief, these women simply sought to do one final service of love for him whom they had followed so faithfully, even to his grave.

Mary Magdalene is the only woman named in all four gospel accounts of the resurrection. However, in John's Gospel, Mary is the first witness to the risen Christ, and her moving encounter with Jesus conveys the pure joy she must have felt as she recognized her master.

Mary came to the tomb early on the first day of the week, as soon as the sabbath had ended. Distressed at not finding Jesus' body there as expected, she ran to tell Simon Peter that it had been removed (John 20:1-2). On her return to the empty tomb, two angels questioned why she was weeping. However,

consumed by grief, she persisted in her assumption that the body had been taken away—perhaps stolen by grave robbers (20:11-13). When Jesus himself stood near her, Mary even mistook him for the caretaker of the garden where the tomb was located (20:14-15).

How is it that Mary—who knew the one who had freed her from her demonic affliction so well—failed to recognize her beloved Lord? Perhaps her tears blinded her. She may have been so overwhelmed by sorrow that she was deceived by her own expectations, with no room in her heart to comprehend any other possibility than that of finding his corpse. Or maybe Jesus' resurrected body was so totally and gloriously transformed that he was unrecognizable.

As if to probe Mary's desire for him, Jesus asked, "Whom do you seek?" (John 20:15). Was she searching for the Lord or, with her limited understanding, for her preconceived image of him as she assumed him to be? When he said "Mary," it was to his voice speaking her name that she finally responded with joyful recognition (20:16). The noted French writer Henri Daniel-Rops described this meeting vividly:

Then the unknown man spoke one word, "Mary," and she looked at him, transfixed. . . . This one word sufficed to reawaken in the Magdalene the ardor and certainty of her faith. What Christian has not dreamed of hearing it, the word with which, from all eternity, God calls each one of us, but which the deaf do not hear. (*Jesus and His Times*)

With this single word, Jesus freed Mary again, this time from the hopelessness that had taken hold of her when she watched him die on the cross. The liturgical prayer known as the sequence, recited at Mass on Easter Monday, poetically imagines Mary's early morning visit to the garden where Jesus was buried: "'Tell us, Mary, what did you see on the way?' 'I saw the tomb of the now living Christ. I saw the glory of Christ, now risen. Christ my hope has risen!'"

When Mary heard her name, she turned and saw the Lord. In a surge of joy and relief she exclaimed, "Rabboni!"—an ecstatic pledge of her faith in Jesus and in his resurrection.

Mary Magdalene, the first to see the risen and glorified Lord, is most remembered for her Easter testimony. Present among the Galilean followers, at the crucifixion, and at the empty tomb, she was an eyewitness to the ministry, death, burial, and resurrection of Jesus. Perhaps she and the other women who shared the suffering at Golgotha and the joy of the resurrection supported one another in the coming years—and shared their memories with the believers who made up the early church. Some early writings state that Mary Magdalene later went to Ephesus with John and the mother of Jesus and was buried there.

In the Latin Church Mary Magdalene is known as *apostola apostolorum* or "female apostle to the male apostles." When she proclaimed "I have seen the Lord!", she was the first to convey the good news to the band of men who had been the closest to Jesus (John 20:18; see also Mark 16:9-10). Mary had accompanied Jesus from village to village, from Galilee to Jerusalem. With ardent love and perseverance, she had even followed him to Golgotha and the tomb. Her faith and constancy were rewarded on that first Easter morning, and she continued to follow Jesus as her risen and victorious Lord. Like Mary Magdalene, we too are called—each of us by name—to follow this same Lord and to share in his resurrection life.

Pondering the Word

1. How would you describe Mary Magdalene's character and personality, based on the information given about her in these gospel scenes: Luke 8:1-3; John 19:25; 20:1-18? Which verses especially indicate ways that she expressed her love for Jesus?

_____

_____

_____

_____

_____

_____

_____

_____

_____

2. What did Simon Peter and the disciple "whom Jesus loved" see when they entered the tomb? Compare John's description of the burial cloths in Jesus' tomb (John 20:5-7) with his description of Jesus raising Lazarus from the dead (11:43-44). What do the differences in these two resurrections suggest to you?

_____

_____

_____

_____

_____

_____

_____

_____

_____

3. What do you think the risen Jesus' appearance was like? Read Luke 24:36-42, John 20:19-20, and 1 Corinthians 15:42-44, 51-53 for additional descriptions of the physical resurrection of the body.

_____

_____

_____

_____

_____

_____

_____

_____

_____

4. Why do you think Mary Magdalene failed at first to recognize Jesus? Describe the sequence of changes in her emotions as her encounter with Jesus unfolded. What does this suggest to you about faith?

_____

_____

_____

_____

_____

_____

_____

_____

_____

5. Compare Mary's encounter with the risen Lord with the encounter between the two disciples and Jesus on the road to Emmaus (Luke 24:13-35). What similarities do you find
in these two scenes?

_____

_____

_____

_____

_____

_____

_____

_____

6. What commission did Jesus give to Mary? Why do you think he chose her to do this?

_____

_____

_____

_____

_____

_____

_____

_____

_____

_____

Living the Word

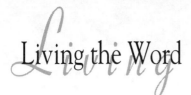

1. What qualities of Mary Magdalene would you like to imitate? Why?

_____

_____

_____

_____

_____

_____

_____

_____

2. Jesus freed Mary from demonic influences in her life. Think of something in your life from which you would like to be freed (perhaps a sin pattern, a negative attitude, an addiction, or a temptation from Satan). Then ask the Lord to free you as he did Mary Magdalene.

_____

_____

_____

_____

_____

_____

_____

_____

3. The women who accompanied Jesus and his disciples showed their love for them in very practical ways. How do you concretely express your love for Jesus? How do you care for or serve your family and fellow Christians?

_____

_____

_____

_____

_____

_____

_____

_____

_____

4. Have your preconceived ideas of where and how Jesus can meet you ever hindered you from recognizing him? When? How were your eyes finally opened to recognize him?

_____

_____

_____

_____

_____

_____

_____

_____

_____

5. Envision the risen Lord appearing to you and calling you by name. When in your life have you felt that the Lord addressed you that personally? How did you respond to him?

_____

_____

_____

_____

_____

_____

_____

_____

_____

6. What effect do you think Jesus' resurrection had on Mary Magdalene's life? What effect does Jesus' resurrection have on your own life? On your eternal perspective?

_____

_____

_____

_____

_____

_____

_____

_____

_____

Rooted in the Word

Mary Magdalene: A Portrait of Love Stronger than Death

In the Old Testament, God's love for his people was reflected in the covenant he made with them. The prophets often described this covenant as a betrothal or compared it to the relationship between a husband and his bride. In the New Testament, God's covenant was fulfilled in Jesus, who is the fullness of the Father's love: "God so loved the world that he gave his only Son, that whoever believes in him should not perish but have eternal life" (John 3:16).

Mary Magdalene's love for Jesus knew no limits. She had experienced his love and its power when he drove seven demons away from her, and she responded with a grateful, loving heart. So great was her devotion to Jesus that she accompanied him as he went about his ministry and braved the horror of Golgotha to stand faithfully by him as he was crucified. Even when her beloved Lord was laid in the tomb, Mary's love did not die. Indeed, her ardor grew more intense when his body was not to be found, and she sought it with longing.

Mary's love was stronger than death, enduring beyond the grave. Her seeking and her love were rewarded with the appearance of her risen Lord—and, ultimately, with the joy of beholding him and loving him forever in heaven.

Through Jesus Christ, God lavishes his love on each of us—and Mary Magdalene offers us an example of how to love him in return. When St. Bernard of Clairvaux was once asked why and how much God should be loved, he replied, "My answer is that God himself is the reason why he should be loved. As for how he is to be loved, there is to be no limit to that love." May our love for Jesus be as limitless and as immeasurable as Mary's!

Read and prayerfully reflect on these additional Scripture passages that describe God's love and the love of those who ardently long for him:

> O God, thou art my God, I seek thee,
>   my soul thirsts for thee;
> my flesh faints for thee,
>   as in a dry and weary land
>   where no water is.
> So I have looked upon thee in the
>   sanctuary,
>   beholding thy power and glory.
> Because thy steadfast love is better
>   than life,
>   my lips will praise thee.
> So I will bless thee as long as I live;
>   I will lift up my hands and call on
>   thy name.
> (Psalm 63:1-4)

Set me as a seal upon your heart,
    as a seal upon your arm;
for love is strong as death.
(Song of Solomon 8:6)

I will greatly rejoice in the LORD,
    my soul shall exult in my God;
for he has clothed me with the
        garments of salvation,
    he has covered me with the robe of
        righteousness,
as a bridegroom decks himself with
        a garland,
    and as a bride adorns herself with
        her jewels.
For as a young man marries a virgin,
    so shall your sons marry you,
and as the bridegroom rejoices
        over the bride,
    so shall your God rejoice over you.
(Isaiah 61:10; 62:5)

In that day, says the LORD, ". . . I will betroth you to me for ever; I will betroth
you to me in righteousness and in justice,
in steadfast love, and in mercy. I will betroth you to me in faithfulness; and you
shall know the LORD." (Hosea 2:19-20)

If God is for us, who is against us? He
who did not spare his own Son but gave
him up for us all, will he not also give us
all things with him? Who shall bring any
charge against God's elect? It is God who
justifies; who is to condemn? Is it Christ
Jesus, who died, yes, who was raised
from the dead, who is at the right hand
of God, who indeed intercedes for us?
Who shall separate us from the love of
Christ? Shall tribulation, or distress, or
persecution, or famine, or nakedness,
or peril, or sword? . . . No, in all these
things we are more than conquerors
through him who loved us. For I am sure
that neither death, nor life, nor angels,
nor principalities, nor things present, nor
things to come, nor powers, nor height,
nor depth, nor anything else in all cre-
ation, will be able to separate us from the
love of God in Christ Jesus our Lord.
(Romans 8:31-35, 37-39)

In this the love of God was made man-
ifest among us, that God sent his only
Son into the world, so that we might live
through him. In this is love, not that we
loved God but that he loved us and
sent his Son to be the expiation for our
sins. Beloved, if God so loved us, we also
ought to love one another. No man has
ever seen God; if we love one another,
God abides in us and his love is perfected
in us. (1 John 4:9-12)

Treasuring the Word

A Reading from a Homily on the Gospels by St. Gregory the Great

She Longed for Christ, Though She Thought He Had Been Taken Away

When Mary Magdalene came to the tomb and did not find the Lord's body, she thought it had been taken away and so informed the disciples. After they came and saw the tomb, they too believed what Mary had told them. The text then says: *The disciples went back home*, and it adds: *but Mary wept and remained standing outside the tomb.*

We should reflect on Mary's attitude and the great love she felt for Christ; for though the disciples had left the tomb, she remained. She was still seeking the one she had not found, and while she sought she wept; burning with the fire of love, she longed for him who she thought had been taken way. And so it happened that the woman who stayed behind to seek Christ was the only one to see him. For perseverance is essential to any good deed, as the voice of truth tells us: *Whoever perseveres to the end will be saved.*

At first she sought but did not find, but when she persevered it happened that she found what she was looking for. When our desires are not satisfied, they grow stronger, and becoming stronger they take hold of their object. Holy desires likewise grow with anticipation, and if they do not grow they are not really desires. Anyone who succeeds in attaining the truth has burned with such a love. As David says: *My soul has thirsted for the living God; when shall I come and appear before the face of God?* And so also in the Song of Songs the Church says: *I was wounded by love*; and again: *My soul is melted with love.*

Woman, why are you weeping? Whom do you seek? She is asked why she is sorrowing so that her desire might be strengthened; for when she mentions whom she is seeking, her love is kindled all the more ardently.

Jesus says to her: Mary. Jesus is not recognized when he calls her "woman"; so he calls her by name, as though he were saying: Recognize me as I recognize you; for I do not know you as I know others; I know you as yourself. And so Mary, once addressed by name, recognizes who is speaking. She immediately calls him *rabboni*, that is to say, *teacher*, because the one whom she sought outwardly was the one who inwardly taught her to keep on searching.

Thomas

My Lord and my God!
John 20:28

In one burning
utterance, Thomas
gathered up all of the
doubts of a depressed
humanity to have them
healed by the full
implications of the
exclamation, "My Lord
and my God."
Archbishop Fulton Sheen,
Life of Christ

Graven on the Palms of Your Hands

Long ago, my Lord and God,
your hands clung 'round Mary's neck,
tiny fingers twining her hair about them
while she hugged you to her breast.
Later Joseph held your boy-hand secure within his firm grasp
as you walked the road together on your first pilgrimage to Jerusalem.
Deftly, too, your hands learned from his to handle lathe
and plane rough wood beams to smoothness.

With sure hand (and a touch that blessed and healed)
you tousled the curly heads of the children who flocked around you,
and opened the blind man's eyes, giving sight again.
(I wonder, too, what that hand wrote in the dust,
disquieting the elders who'd hoped to ensnare you
in the trap they'd laid for the adulteress.)

Raised in thanksgiving,
your hands
multiplied the loaves and fishes
and broke the bread
that fed your disciples' hunger with more than crushed wheat.

Then those same hands
that washed soiled feet
(and stained, sin-encrusted souls)
were wrenched and held fast,
forced to the crossbeam as the executioner plied open your fingers
and drove iron through your palms,
inscribing my name upon them:

Behold, I have graven you on the palms of my hands.

Tendons mangled and severed,
nerves vibrating in agony,
muscles contorted in tight spasms—
those hands were made useless
except to hold you pinioned to the cross
as your body sagged,
its weight straining and pressing raw against the nails.

Then gloriously risen from the grave,
you showed those same pierced hands to Thomas,
inviting him to probe the nail marks
and overcome all doubt and incredulity:

Do not be faithless but believing.

Your hands, once so wounded and so bloodied,
still bear the hard-won battle scars—
signs of victory and glory
and a record of the price you paid for me.

And now you never cease
to intercede before the throne of God,
those wounds indelibly written upon your flesh
pleading there on my behalf.

John 20:19-20, 24-29

20:19 On the evening of that day, the first day of the week, the doors being shut where the disciples were, for fear of the Jews, Jesus came and stood among them and said to them, "Peace be with you." 20 When he had said this, he showed them his hands and his side. Then the disciples were glad when they saw the Lord.

24 Now Thomas, one of the twelve, called the Twin, was not with them when Jesus came. 25 So the other disciples told him, "We have seen the Lord." But he said to them, "Unless I see in his hands the print of the nails, and place my finger in the mark of the nails, and place my hand in his side, I will not believe."

26 Eight days later, his disciples were again in the house, and Thomas was with them. The doors were shut, but Jesus came and stood among them, and said, "Peace be with you." 27 Then he said to Thomas, "Put your finger here, and see my hands; and put out your hand, and place it in my side; do not be faithless, but believing." 28 Thomas answered him, "My Lord and my God!" 29 Jesus said to him, "Have you believed because you have seen me? Blessed are those who have not seen and yet believe."

See also John 11:5-16

Reflecting on the Word

Thomas knew with a certainty that Jesus was dead. All of Jerusalem knew that the rabbi from Galilee had been crucified and hastily buried. How then, he reasoned logically, could he possibly give any credence to the other disciples' report that Jesus had returned to life and appeared to them (John 20:19-20, 24-25; see also Luke 24:36-43)? Though Thomas was a brave man, one who had been ready to accompany Jesus into danger when the Pharisees were hunting him (John 11:8, 16), he was also a realist who moved only when he was sure of the way to go (14:5). He was a man who would only believe what he could see with his own eyes, who wanted to handle the evidence with his own hands before he would be convinced of anything and commit himself to it wholeheartedly. Thus, it's become common in colloquial speech to refer to a skeptic as a "Doubting Thomas."

Thomas set stringent conditions for belief—"Unless I see in [Jesus'] hands the print of the nails, and place my finger in the mark of the nails, and place my hand in his side, I will not believe" (John 20:25). Given these strong terms, we might think him callous and faithless. Yet Jesus had first shown his wounded hands and feet to the other disciples as proof of his identity and to calm their fear: "Why are you troubled, and why do questionings arise in your hearts? See my hands and my feet, that it is I myself; handle me and see: for a spirit has not flesh and bones as you

see that I have" (Luke 24:38-39). Absent on that occasion, Thomas had heard his friends' report of it (John 20:24). Finding it hard to believe that Jesus was indeed alive, he demanded the same assurance the others had been offered.

Once Thomas saw Jesus with his own eyes, his response was total surrender and belief. He was convinced and overwhelmed, perhaps not so much by the proof he saw in Jesus' wounded hands and side as by the love and understanding that Jesus had for him. This risen Lord had already known Thomas' thoughts and unhesitatingly offered the doubter his wounded side. A striking description of this encounter is given by Ronald Brownrigg in *Who's Who in the Bible:*

> In that moment Thomas must have seen both the body on the cross, hanging by hands and feet, the side opened by the soldier's spear, and his living friend and master. As these two figures fused together, so Thomas leapt the gap between loyalty to a friend and adoring faith in God himself. His ponderous pessimism and lonely doubts disappeared, and he identified his friend as both "My Lord and my God!"

Kyrios theos—"My Lord and my God!" (John 20:28)—is the Greek translation used for *Yahweh 'Elôhîm*, the Hebrew term for the God of Israel. In Thomas' mouth, it's also a complete acknowledgment of Christ's nature and one of the most definitive assertions of faith recorded in the gospels. With this response, Thomas left no room for doubt of Jesus' identity. Since he realized that Jesus had read his heart and known of his bold demand, his reply was not just a profession of faith but an act of adoration and an expression of deep sorrow at his own brashness and unbelief.

Scripture scholars note that the Gospel of John originally ended with the account of Thomas' encounter with the risen Lord and his proclamation of faith. (Chapter 21, considered by most scholars to be a later addition to John's Gospel, has been fully accepted in the canon of Scripture since the earliest days of the Church even though it may not have been written by John himself.) Through Thomas' proclamation of faith, John was affirming Jesus' resurrection for his readers and establishing it as a fact. The evangelist concluded his work with the statement that he had written his Gospel so that his readers would come to the same belief in the Messiah as Thomas did and have life in Jesus' name (John 20:31).

Just as Jesus was gracious to Thomas, he is gracious to us. Thomas' doubts serve to confirm our own faith in the risen Lord, noted St. Gregory the Great in his *Homilies on the Gospels*, and his testimony strengthens our belief:

Do you really believe that it was by chance that this chosen disciple was absent, then came and heard, heard and doubted, doubted and touched, touched and believed? It was not by chance but in God's providence. In a marvelous way God's mercy arranged that the disbelieving disciple, in touching the wounds of his master's body, should heal our wounds of disbelief. The disbelief of Thomas has done more for our faith than the faith of the other disciples. As he touches Christ and is won over to belief, every doubt is cast aside and our faith is strengthened. So the disciple who doubted, then felt Christ's wounds, becomes a witness to the reality of the resurrection.

Jesus readily gave Thomas the assurance that he had sought by being physically present to the doubter and showing his wounds to him. But he especially commended those whose belief was gained through faith rather than sight: "Blessed are those who have not seen and yet believe" (John 20:29). As St. Gregory further explained,

Faith is the proof of what cannot be seen. What is seen gives knowledge, not faith. When Thomas saw and touched, why was he told: *You have believed because you have seen me?* Because what he saw and what he believed were different things. God cannot be seen by mortal man. Thomas saw a human being, whom he acknowledged to be God, and said: *My Lord and my God.* Seeing, he believed; looking at one who was true man, he cried out that this was God, the God he could not see.

What follows is reason for great joy: *Blessed are those who have not seen and have believed.* There is here a particular reference to ourselves; we hold in our hearts one we have not seen in the flesh. We are included in these words. . . .

Peter, who was probably present at this scene, later encouraged Christians who had become believers with words similar to those Jesus had spoken to Thomas: "Without having seen him you love him; though you do not now see him you believe in him and rejoice with unutterable and exalted joy. As the outcome of your faith you obtain the salvation of your souls" (1 Peter 1:8-9). Blessed are we, too, when we believe without seeing! Jesus' resurrected body "possesses the new properties of a glorious body: not limited by space and time but able to be present how and when he wills" (*Catechism of the Catholic Church,* 645). With this body that had been tortured, crucified, and raised from the dead, he was able to pass through locked doors (John 20:19) and eat fish (Luke 24:42-43). Yet Jesus' glorified body retained its wound marks as a sign of the high price paid for our redemption.

These wounds are still visible as Jesus, the lamb slain for us, stands glorified before the Father (Revelation 5:6). Reflecting on the wounds of Christ, St. Ambrose wrote,

> He chose to bring to heaven those wounds he bore for us, he refused to remove them, so that he might show God the Father the price of our freedom. The Father places him in this state at his right hand, embracing the trophy of our salvation: such are the witnesses the crown of his scars has shown us there.

Tradition tells us that Thomas' love for his crucified and risen Lord later led him to carry the good news to India, where he died a martyr's death by the spear.

Pondering the Word

1. What do Jesus' wounds indicate to you about his risen body? Describe some of the other properties of Jesus' body after the resurrection. Why do you think the evangelists emphasized these qualities so much?

_____

_____

_____

_____

_____

_____

_____

_____

2. Do you think Thomas' request was unreasonable? Why or why not? In what tone of voice or with what attitude do you imagine he said it? Bewildered? Challenging? Tentative and searching? Demanding?

_____

_____

_____

_____

_____

_____

_____

_____

3. Describe the steps that Thomas took from unbelief to belief. What does this progression suggest to you about growing in faith?

_____

_____

_____

_____

_____

_____

_____

_____

4. What insights into the connection between faith and the fellowship and support of believers does this story give you?

_____

_____

_____

_____

_____

_____

_____

_____

5. Does faith depend on sight? If not, what is the basis of faith? Explain Jesus' statement, "Blessed are those who have not seen and yet believe" (John 20:29).

_____

_____

_____

_____

_____

_____

_____

_____

6. Can you think of others in the gospels who asked for "proof" before they could or would believe in God's word and his ability to fulfill it? Of some people who didn't need any proof to convince them?

_____

_____

_____

_____

_____

_____

_____

_____

Living the Word

1. Imagine yourself in Thomas' place. Would you have believed the other disciples' report? How do you think you would have responded to seeing the risen Lord?

_____

_____

_____

_____

_____

_____

_____

_____

_____

2. What kind of demands have you, like Thomas, put on God to prove himself to you or to assure you of his love? Why?

_____

_____

_____

_____

_____

_____

_____

_____

_____

3. Do you find it challenging to believe in God because you can't see him? Write a short prayer asking God to reveal himself to you more clearly (perhaps through Scripture, through other people, in nature) and to strengthen your faith.

_____

_____

_____

_____

_____

_____

_____

_____

_____

4. How do you deal with doubts to your faith? Do you ignore them or try to resolve them? Can you recall a person whose faith was a strong support to you when your own faith was weak?

_____

_____

_____

_____

_____

_____

_____

_____

_____

5. The other apostles sought to convince Thomas that Jesus had risen and appeared to them. When has your faith in the risen Lord impelled you to share the gospel with others? What experiences have you had of helping bring another person to faith in Jesus?

_____

_____

_____

_____

_____

_____

_____

_____

6. What practical steps can you take to nurture and safeguard your faith?

_____

_____

_____

_____

_____

_____

_____

_____

Rooted in the Word

Thomas: A Portrait of a Believing Heart

Thomas was not the only one who was a doubter. Jesus had encountered many who refused to believe in him. Their hearts hardened against him, they failed to recognize that he had been sent to them from God to bring salvation and redemption.

The Pharisees and Sadducees tested Jesus, demanding to see a sign from him (Matthew 16:1-4). Before healing the boy, Jesus told the official whose son was near death, "Unless you see signs and wonders you will not believe" (John 4:48). To the crowds who wondered that Jesus called himself the bread of life, he said, "You have seen me and yet do not believe" (6:36). At Jesus' crucifixion, the chief priests and scribes mocked him, saying, "Let the Christ, the King of Israel, come down now from the cross, that we may see and believe" (Mark 15:32).

Thomas wanted proof before he would believe that Jesus had returned to life. But when he encountered the risen Lord, his eyes saw more than a body that gave evidence of both its wounds and its glorification—Thomas saw with his heart and recognized in Jesus his Lord and Savior. His reverent and joyful exclamation, "My Lord and my God!" is a profound profession of faith.

Thomas had doubted, but once he believed, he was wholehearted about his faith. Tradition knows him as the apostle to India, where he zealously spread the gospel and gave witness—even by martyrdom—to the risen Christ.

Read and prayerfully reflect on these additional Scripture passages that illustrate the importance and outcome of having faith-filled and believing hearts:

Jesus said to them, "I am the bread of life; he who comes to me shall not hunger, and he who believes in me shall never thirst. But I said to you that you have seen me and yet do not believe. All that the Father gives me will come to me; and him who comes to me I will not cast out. For I have come down from heaven, not to do my own will, but the will of him who sent me; and this is the will of him who sent me, that I should lose nothing of all that he has given me, but raise it up at the last day. For this is the will of my Father, that every one who sees the Son and believes in him should have eternal life; and I will raise him up at the last day." (John 6:35-40)

Jesus said to [Martha], "I am the resurrection and the life; he who believes in me, though he die, yet shall he live, and whoever lives and believes in me shall never die. Do you believe this?" (John 11:25-26)

Jesus cried out and said, "He who believes in me, believes not in me but in him who sent me. And he who sees me sees him who sent me. I have come as light into the world, that whoever believes in me may not remain in darkness." (John 12:44-46)

[Jesus said:] "Truly, truly, I say to you, he who believes in me will also do the works that I do; and greater works than these will he do, because I go to the Father." (John 14:12)

If you confess with your lips that Jesus is Lord and believe in your heart that God raised him from the dead, you will be saved. For man believes with his heart and so is justified, and he confesses with his lips and so is saved. The scripture says, "No one who believes in him will be put to shame." For there is no distinction between Jew and Greek; the same Lord is Lord of all and bestows his riches upon all who call upon him. For, "every one who calls upon the name of the Lord will be saved." (Romans 10:9-13)

For since we believe that Jesus died and rose again, even so, through Jesus, God will bring with him those who have fallen asleep. (1 Thessalonians 4:14)

Treasuring the Word

A Reading from *The Inner Life of Jesus* by Romano Guardini

Recognizing the Presence of Jesus

There was one of the twelve, Thomas, who is also called Didymus, who was not with them when Jesus came. And when the other disciples told him, "We have seen the Lord," he said to them, "Until I have seen the marks of the nails on His hands, until I have put my finger into the mark of the nails, and put my hand into His side, you will never make me believe." Thomas appears to have been a realist: reserved, cool, and perhaps a little obstinate.

The days went by, and the disciples went on living under this considerable tension. After a week, they were together again in the house, and this time Thomas was with them. The same thing repeated itself. Jesus passed through the closed doors, stepped into their midst, and spoke: "Peace be upon you." Then He called the man who was struggling against faith: "Let me have thy finger; see, here are my hands. Let me have thy hand; put it into my side. Cease thy doubting, and believe!" At this point, Thomas was overwhelmed. The truth of it all came home to him: this man standing before him, so moving, arousing such deep feelings within him, this man so full of mystery, so different from all other men—

He is the very same one they used to be together with, who was put to death a short time ago. And Thomas surrendered: "Thou art my Lord and my God!" Thomas believed.

Then we come upon the strange words: "And Jesus said to him, 'Thou hast learned to believe, Thomas, because thou hast seen me. Blessed are those who have not seen, and yet have learned to believe.'"

Such words as these are really extraordinary! Thomas believed because he saw. But our Lord did not call him blessed. He had been allowed to see—to see the hands and the side, and to touch the blessed wounds, yet he was not blessed!

Perhaps Thomas had a narrow escape from a great danger. He wanted proofs, wanted to see and touch; but then, too, it might have been rebellion deep within him, the vainglory of an intelligence that would not surrender, a sluggishness and coldness of heart. He got what he asked for: a look and a touch. But it must have been a concession he deplored having received, when he thought on it afterward. He could have believed and been saved, not because he got what he demanded; he could have believed because God's mercy had touched his heart and given him the grace of interior vision, the gift of the opening of the heart, and of its surrender.

God could also have let him stay with the words he had spoken: in that state of unbelief which cuts itself off from everything, that insists on human evidence to become convinced. In that case, he would have remained an unbeliever and gone on his way. In that state, external seeing and touching would not have helped him at all; he simply would have called it delusion. Nothing that comes from God, even the greatest miracle, proves out like two times two. It touches a person; it is only seen and grasped when the heart is open and the spirit is purged of self. Then it awakens faith. But when these conditions are not present, there are always reasons to be found to say solemnly and impressively that it is all delusion, or that such-and-such is so because some other thing is so. Or, the excuse that is always handy: We cannot explain it yet; the future will enlighten us about it.

Thomas was standing a hair's breadth away from obduracy and perdition. He was not at all blessed.

Blessed indeed are "those who have not seen, and yet have learned to believe." Those who ask for no miracles, demand nothing out of the ordinary, but who find God's message in everyday life. Those who require no compelling proofs, but who know that everything coming from God must remain in a certain ultimate suspense, so that faith may never cease to require daring. Those who know that the heart is not overcome by faith, that there is no force or violence there, compelling belief by rigid certitudes. What comes from God touches gently, comes quietly, does not disturb freedom, and leads to quiet, profound, peaceful resolve within the heart. And those are called blessed who make the effort to remain open-hearted; who seek to cleanse their hearts of all self-righteousness, obstinacy, presumption, and inclination to "know better"; who are quick to hear, humble, and free-spirited. Those are called blessed who are able to find God's message in the Gospel for the day, or even from the sermons of preachers with no message in particular; or in phrases from the Law they have heard a thousand times, phrases of no quality of charismatic power about them; or in the happenings of everyday life which always end up the same way: work and rest, anxiety—and then again some kind of success, some joy, an encounter, and a sorrow.

Blessed are those who can see the Lord in all these things!

Source Notes and Acknowledgments

This section indicates the sources of material quoted in
My Lord and My God! A Scriptural Journey with the Followers of Jesus.

Introduction

Page 6:
Richard of Chicester, quoted in
The Catholic Prayer Book,
compiled by Msgr. Michael
Buckley (Ann Arbor, Mich.:
Servant Books, 1986), p. 152.

Page 7:
Josemaría Escrivá, quoted in
Francis Fernandez, *In Conversation with God–Volume Two*
(London: Scepter Ltd., 1989),
pp. 347–348 and p. 455.

Reflection 1: Simon Peter

Page 10:
C. Bernard Ruffin, *The Twelve:
The Lives of the Apostles After
Calvary* (Huntington, Ind.: Our
Sunday Visitor Publishing
Division, 1997), p. 23.

Page 14:
Ruffin, p. 23.

Page 15:
Sister Wendy Beckett, *Sister
Wendy's Nativity* (Chicago:
Loyola Press, 1998), p. 66.

Louise Perrotta, "From
Fisherman to Friend of God,"
The Word Among Us Magazine,
Lent 2003 (Ijamsville, Md.: The
Word Among Us), p. 71.

Page 16:
Perrotta, p. 71.

Page 23:
George T. Montague, S.M.,
Mark: Good News for Hard Times
(Ann Arbor, Mich.: Servant
Books, 1981), p. 22.

Pages 25–27:
Irene Zimmerman, O.S.F.,
Woman Un-Bent (Winona,
Minn.: St. Mary's Press, 1999),
pp. 101–103. Reprinted with
permission of the author.

Reflection 2: The Centurion of Capernaum

Page 28:
Augustine, *Sermons on Selected
Lessons of the New Testament*,
Sermon XII. Available on the
Internet: http://www.newadvent
.org/fathers/160312.htm.

Page 31:
Polybius, *History*, Book VI, 24.
Available on the Internet:
http://www.wcg.org/lit/bible/acts/
acts10.htm.

Page 32:
Ambrose, quoted in Thomas
Aquinas, *Catena Aurea* (The
Golden Chain), Luke 7:1-10.
Available on the Internet:
http://members.wri.com/billw/
blog/archives/000183.shtml.

Page 33:
Fulton J. Sheen, *Life of Christ*
(New York: Image Books, 1990),
p. 232.

Pages 42–43:
John Eudes Bamberger,
O.C.S.O., "Lord, I Am Not
Worthy." Homily given on
September 13, 1999. Copyright
© Abbey of the Genesee.
Reprinted with permission of
the author. Available on the
Internet: http://www
.abbotjohneudes.org/h13sept99
.html.

Reflection 3: The Woman with the Hemorrhage

Page 44:
Ambrose, quoted in *The Navarre
Bible: The Gospel of St. Mark*,
with a commentary by the
members of the Faculty of
Theology of the University of
Navarre (Blackrock, Ireland:
Four Courts Press, 1992), p. 101.

Page 49:
Montague, p. 68.

Page 56:
Teresa of Avila, quoted in *The
Voice of the Saints*, selected and
arranged by Francis W. Johnston
(Rockford, Ill.: Tan Books and
Publishers, Inc.), p. 129.

Jane de Chantal, quoted in *A
Dictionary of Quotes from the
Saints*, compiled by Paul Thigpen
(Ann Arbor, Mich.: Servant
Publications, 2001), p. 237.

Page 58–59:
Ann Spangler and Jean E.
Syswerda, *Women of the Bible: A*

One-Year Devotional Study of Women in Scripture (Grand Rapids, Mich.: Zondervan Publishing House, 1999), pp. 333–334. Copyright © 1999 by Ann Spangler and Jean Syswerda. Reprinted with permission of The Zondervan Corporation.

Reflection 4: Zacchaeus

Page 60:
Ambrose, quoted in Francis Fernandez, In Conversation with God–Volume Five (London: Scepter Ltd., 1997), pp. 376–377.

Page 73:
John Paul II, quoted in Fernandez, In Conversation with God–Volume Five, p. 375.

Catechism of the Catholic Church (San Francisco: Ignatius Press), 1432 and 1431, p. 360.

Pages 75-76:
John Paul II, Letter to Priests for Holy Thursday 2002, 4–7. Promulgated 17 March 2002. Available on the Internet: http://www.vatican.va/holy _father/john_paul_ii/letters/ 2002/documents/hf_jp-ii_let _20020321_priests-holy -thursday_en.html.

Reflection 5: Bartimaeus

Page 78:
John Chrysostom, quoted in The Navarre Bible: The Gospel of St. Mark, p. 147.

Page 82:
Philip Van Linden, quoted in The Collegeville Bible Commentary, ed.

Dianne Bergant, C.S.A., and Robert Karris, O.F.M. (Collegeville, Minn.: The Liturgical Press, 1989), p. 925.

Page 83:
Josemaría Escrivá, quoted in The Navarre Bible: The Gospel of St. Mark, p. 147.

Page 90:
The Navarre Bible: The Gospel of St. Luke, with a commentary by the members of the Faculty of Theology of the University of Navarre (Blackrock, Ireland: Four Courts Press, 1993), p. 207.

Thomas Aquinas, quoted in Francis Fernandez, In Conversation with God–Volume Three (London: Scepter Ltd., 1990), p. 263.

Pages 93–94:
Josemaría Escrivá, Friends of God (London and New York: Scepter Ltd., 1990), pp. 174–177. English translation copyright ©1981, 1986 by Scepter Ltd. Reprinted with permission of Scepter Publishers, P.O. Box 211, New York, New York 10018.

Reflection 6: Mary of Bethany

Page 96:
Alfred McBride, O. Praem., The Divine Presence of Jesus: Meditation and Commentary on the Gospel of John (Huntington, Ind.: Our Sunday Visitor Publishing Division, 1992), pp. 110–111.

Pages 100–101:
M. Basilea Schlink, The Holy Places Today (Darmstadt-Eberstadt, Germany: Evangelical Sisterhood of Mary, 1975), p. 19.

Page 102:
John Chrysostom, quoted in The Navarre Bible: The Gospel of St. Mark, p. 170.

Pages 111–112:
Adrienne von Speyr, Three Women and the Lord (San Francisco: Ignatius Press, 1986), pp. 86–88. Copyright © 1986 by Ignatius Press. Reprinted with permission of Ignatius Press.

Reflection 7: Judas

Page 114:
Fernandez, In Conversation with God–Volume Two, p. 244.

Page 118:
Sheen, p. 291.

Pages 118–119 :
McBride, The Divine Presence of Jesus, p. 123.

Page 119:
Beckett, p. 62.

Leo the Great, Letters and Sermons, Sermon 67. Available on the Internet: http://ww2 .netnitco.net/users/legend01/ torch.htm.

Page 120:
Beckett, p. 62.

Page 127:
Alfred McBride, O. Praem., The Kingdom and the Glory: Meditation and Commentary on the Gospel of Matthew (Huntington, Ind.: Our Sunday Visitor Publishing Division, 1992), p. 153.

Catechism, 1429, p. 359.

Pages 129–130:
Ralph Martin, *Who Do You Say I Am?* (Ann Arbor, Mich.: Servant Ministries, 1989), pp. 6–11. Copyright © 1989 by Ralph Martin. Reprinted with permission of the author.

Reflection 8: Joseph of Arimathea and Nicodemus

Page 132:
F.J. Sheed, *To Know Christ Jesus* (San Francisco: Ignatius Press, 1992), pp. 365–366.

Pages 136–137:
Luis de la Palma, quoted in Fernandez, *In Conversation with God–Volume Two*, pp. 289–290.

Page 137:
Augustine, quoted in *Stephen Ray, St. John's Gospel: A Bible Study Guide and Commentary* (San Francisco: Ignatius Press, 2000), p. 364.

Page 145:
Ignatius of Loyola, *Prayer for Generosity*. Available on the Internet: http://feastofsaints .com/threeofignatius.htm.

Pages 148–149:
Fulton J. Sheen, *Life of Christ* (New York: Image Books, 1990), pp. 400–401. Copyright © 1958, 1977 by Fulton J. Sheen. Reprinted with permission of Doubleday, a division of Random House, Inc.

Reflection 9: Mary Magdalene

Page 150:
Fernandez, *In Conversation with God–Volume Two*, p. 306.

Pages 156–157:
Henri Daniel-Rops, *Jesus and His Times, Volume Two* (Garden City, N.Y.: Image Books, 1958), pp. 240–241.

Pages 157:
Sequence, Monday of the Octave of Easter, quoted in *Saint Joseph Weekday Missal, Volume I* (New York: Catholic Book Publishing Co., 1975), p. 769.

Page 164:
Bernard of Clairvaux, *Love Songs: Wisdom from Saint Bernard of Clairvaux*, ed. Jeanne Kun (Ijamsville, Md.: The Word Among Us Press, 2001), p. 31. Sheen, p. 259.

Pages 166:
Gregory the Great, quoted in *The Liturgy of the Hours, Volume III* (New York: Catholic Book Publishing Co., 1975), pp. 1543–44. English translation copyright © 1974 by International Commission on English in the Liturgy, Inc. All rights reserved. Reprinted with permission of The International Commission on English in the Liturgy, Inc.

Reflection 10: Thomas

Page 168:
Sheen, p. 424.

Page 172:
Joan Comay and Ronald Brownrigg, *Who's Who in the Bible* (New York: Bonanza Books, 1980), p. 436.

Pages 173–174:
Gregory the Great, quoted in *The Liturgy of the Hours, Volume III*, pp. 1516–17.

Page 174:
Catechism, 645, p. 168.

Ambrose, "On the Wounds of the Risen Christ." Available on the Internet: http://www .arimathea.co.uk/saint.htm.

Pages 183–184:
Romano Guardini, *The Inner Life of Jesus: Pattern of All Holiness* (Manchester, N. H.: Sophia Institute Press, 1998), pp. 119–122. English translation copyright © 1959 by Regnery Publishing, Inc. All rights reserved. Reprinted by special permission of Regnery Publishing, Inc., Washington, D.C.

Notes

Notes

Notes

Notes

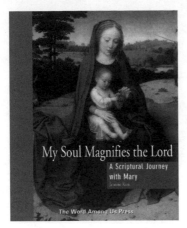

Item # BIGVE3

Also by Jeanne Kun

My Soul Magnifies the Lord
A Scriptural Journey with Mary

Follow in the footsteps of the first disciple of Jesus—his mother Mary. As readers take this pilgrimage of faith, their own faith will deepen along the way! This unique book focuses on ten important gospel scenes in the life of the Blessed Virgin Mary, from her fiat at the Annunciation to her presence in the upper room at Pentecost. Each chapter includes: a poetic meditation; the Scripture passage to be studied; a series of questions for delving deeper into the meaning and significance of each scene; and questions for applying these truths to our own lives.

"By presenting the milestones of Mary's life as recorded in the Bible, this Scripture study can do a great deal to increase its readers' faith and humbleness of heart."
National Catholic Register

"An enticing aid to prayer."
Bible Today

To order call 1-800-775-9673 or order online at www.wordamongus.org